"In church contexts that define
sonality, and technique, Paul's ᴜᴇᴏʟᴏɢy ᴏɪ pastoral ministry in
2 Corinthians is uncomfortably countercultural: humiliating in
transparency about weaknesses, resolute in integrity, and—above
all—exalting Christ instead of self. Pastor Bredenhof's exploration of the glorious gospel paradox—Christ's strength is displayed
through weak pastors, God's priceless treasure conveyed in jars of
clay—will both challenge and encourage pastors in our new covenant ministry. Pastor, whether you are discouraged by criticism
or tempted to self-congratulation by fruitfulness, *Weak Pastor,
Strong Christ* will bring biblical clarity to your view of yourself
and of the service to which your gracious Lord has called you."

—Dennis E. Johnson, professor emeritus of practical
theology, Westminster Seminary California

"Reuben Bredenhof gives us a fine, thoughtful, engaging, and
readable study of 2 Corinthians that opens up the apostle Paul's
pastoral mind and heart to today's pastors and church members.
Those in pastoral ministry will find this book immensely encouraging, realistic, and practical, as will church members. Reuben
both opens up the difficulties and joys Paul experienced in pastoring the Corinthian Christians in the first century and bridges
the gap between then and now so that the importance and relevance of Paul's teaching for today's churches and pastors is clear.
This wise and practical book goes well beyond the superficiality
of 'how to' books on Christian ministry to dig deep into theology
and ministry. Read it—you'll learn much from it!"

—Steve Walton, professor of New Testament, Trinity College, Bristol

"The premise of this book is straightforward: ministers today can
learn much from the ministry of the apostle Paul in first-century
Corinth. No clever but soon-outdated pragmatism here. This is a
book from a seasoned pastor that is solidly grounded in the God-
inspired words of Paul about his pastoral labors in a difficult place.
Any minister who longs to serve the Lord in accordance with His
word will profit from this volume. Laypeople—especially those

who serve as elders or on a pastor search committee—will find it insightful as well. Generous-hearted laypeople would do well to consider providing a copy for their pastor. Any pastor who receives a copy should be grateful for it, for in these pages is much helpful wisdom."

—Donald S. Whitney, professor of biblical spirituality and associate dean, The Southern Baptist Theological Seminary, Louisville, Kentucky and author of *Spiritual Disciplines for the Christian Life*, *Praying the Bible*, and *Family Worship*

"Many books analyze the apostle Paul's theology and missionary work. Reuben Bredenhof examines the ministry of Paul the pastor in his book *Weak Pastor, Strong Christ*. His careful study of 2 Corinthians unfolds an apostolic model for pastoral work. Here, ministers straining under the burden of unbiblical expectations will find relief; those unsure of how to model their ministry will find godly help. He summons all pastors—in joy or trial—to rely upon Christ's all-sufficient grace, saying with Paul, 'When I am weak, then I am strong.'"

—Charles M. Wingard, associate professor of pastoral theology, Reformed Theological Seminary, and author of *Help for the New Pastor*

WEAK PASTOR,
STRONG CHRIST

WEAK PASTOR,
STRONG CHRIST

Developing a Christ-Shaped Gospel Ministry

Reuben Bredenhof

Reformation Heritage Books
Grand Rapids, Michigan

Weak Pastor, Strong Christ
© 2021 by Reuben Bredenhof

Reformation Heritage Books
3070 29th St. SE
Grand Rapids, MI 49512
616-977-0889
orders@heritagebooks.org
www.heritagebooks.org

Unless otherwise indicated, Scripture taken from the New King James Version®. Copyright © 1982 by Thomas Nelson. Used by permission. All rights reserved.

Scripture quotations marked ESV are taken from the ESV® Bible (The Holy Bible, English Standard Version®). ESV® Text Edition: 2016. Copyright © 2001 by Crossway, a publishing ministry of Good News Publishers. Used by permission. All rights reserved.

All italics in Scripture quotations have been added by the author.

Printed in the United States of America
21 22 23 24 25 26/10 9 8 7 6 5 4 3 2 1

Library of Congress Cataloging-in-Publication Data

Names: Bredenhof, Reuben, author.
Title: Weak pastor, strong Christ : developing a Christ-shaped gospel ministry / Reuben Bredenhof.
Description: Grand Rapids, Michigan : Reformation Heritage Books, [2021] | Includes bibliographical references.
Identifiers: LCCN 2020055907 (print) | LCCN 2020055908 (ebook) | ISBN 9781601788429 (paperback) | ISBN 9781601788436 (epub)
Subjects: LCSH: Bible. Corinthians, 2nd—Criticism, interpretation, etc. | Pastoral theology—Biblical teaching. | Pastoral theology—Reformed Church.
Classification: LCC BS2675.6.P45 B74 2021 (print) | LCC BS2675.6.P45 (ebook) | DDC 253—dc23
LC record available at https://lccn.loc.gov/2020055907
LC ebook record available at https://lccn.loc.gov/2020055908

For additional Reformed literature, request a free book list from Reformation Heritage Books at the above regular or email address.

Gratefully dedicated to the pastors
whose faithful preaching, teaching, and care I received
before becoming a pastor myself:

Rev. Dr. James Visscher
Rev. Jack Moesker
Rev. Clarence Stam†

CONTENTS

Acknowledgments ix

Introduction: Searching for a Model of Ministry 1
1. Serving under Pressure 7
2. Building a Ministerial Identity 17
3. Pastoring Like a Father 29
4. Preaching for the Glory of Christ 47
5. Facing a Barrage of Criticism 63
6. Handling Money Wisely 75
7. Suffering Willingly 91
8. Working with a Purpose 107
Afterword: Traveling from the First Century to Today 121

Selected Bibliography 127

ACKNOWLEDGMENTS

An idea for a new book typically has a long period of gestation. The concept of this book has origins that can be traced back almost a dozen years to when I served my first congregation and enrolled part time in some biblical studies courses. While I was pastoring a church in St. Albert, Alberta, Canada, I completed a master of theology degree with a focus on New Testament studies. This was back in 2009. The final component of the degree program was a thesis, which I chose to write on Paul's relationship with the church of Corinth, particularly as he portrays this pastor-congregation bond in 2 Corinthians. It was a project that combined my love for the New Testament with my growing appreciation for the privilege of pastoral ministry, and I relished the several months I was able to devote to researching and writing on Paul as pastor in 2 Corinthians. Thesis accepted and degree granted, I moved on to other projects.

But my dear wife, Rebecca, who often has excellent ideas, suggested already back then that I should do something more with all the work I had completed on 2 Corinthians. "Turn it into a book" was basically what she said. I agreed that the idea had merit, so it went onto the to-do list, where it stayed for about ten years. But at last the opportune time came for me to take my old thesis off the shelf and to give the project another look. Transforming an academic thesis into an accessible book was, of course, far more work than I expected, but I have thoroughly enjoyed the task—and now it is finally done.

I am grateful to have been able to revisit the beautiful truths found on the pages of God's Word in 2 Corinthians, the powerful gospel realities, and the encouraging lessons in gospel ministry. I have certainly not written this book as a minister who has found all the answers and learned all the lessons, but in the deep awareness that I am just one more weak pastor who needs to live in dependence on the strong Christ.

As she has been for many years now, Rebecca was a great support for my work on this book too. With love I thank her for always walking alongside me in my ministry, for reading (twice!) and commenting on all these pages, and, indeed, for giving me that good idea for a book so long ago. Once again, the content of this book needed to pass the careful scrutiny of our daughters—Abigail, Kyra, Sasha, and Tori—who can always be counted on to provide helpful comments, insightful observations, and warm encouragement to their dad. Much appreciation goes to Marlene de Vos of my congregation, who was again ready and willing to spend many hours proofreading an early draft. I would also like to thank the friends and colleagues who happily accepted my invitation to read and comment on the manuscript: Rev. Axel Hagg, Dr. DongWoo Oh, and Rev. Wieste Huizenga. The book is better for their many wise and thoughtful queries and suggestions. Finally, it has been a pleasure to work on this project with Dr. Jay Collier from Reformation Heritage Books and to benefit from the editorial labors of Dr. Drew McGinnis.

May the lessons for ministry drawn from 2 Corinthians be a blessing to all who read these pages!

SEARCHING FOR A MODEL OF MINISTRY

Imitate me, just as I also imitate Christ.
—1 CORINTHIANS 11:1

I was twenty-seven years old, fresh out of seminary with a master of divinity in hand, and just beginning the work of pastoral ministry in a church in central Alberta, Canada. Years of preparation had finally led to getting a job and taking up a meaningful task. But even amid my excitement about the new position and responsibility, I felt a whiff of uncertainty. There were lingering doubts and misgivings about what it would take to do this work properly in the coming years. Old hesitations about personal competence and character were suddenly resurrected and became pronounced in my mind. Seminary supplied certain tools—basic skill in exegesis and sermon crafting, some knowledge of church history, and the fundamentals of human psychology—but still I wondered: How can I actually be a *pastor* in the truest sense of the word, shepherding a congregation effectively and with purpose? How can I work faithfully among the church members who have now been placed in my care?

These questions are not new. For as long as the Christian church has been in existence, there have been persons entrusted with the task of caring for the church's members. And these persons—whether called bishops, overseers, elders, presbyters, ministers, or pastors— have always needed to reflect on their work and to be guided and encouraged in the proper manner of ministry. Already in the first few decades after Christ's time on earth, the apostle Paul gave instruction on pastoral ministry when he wrote two letters to Timothy and one to Titus, men who were involved in the care of Christian congregations. Timothy in particular seems to have struggled with questions of his personal suitability for the task. His struggle is mirrored in Paul's words, "Let no one despise your youth, but be an example to the believers in word, in conduct, in love, in spirit, in faith, in purity" (1 Tim. 4:12). And Paul equipped Timothy and Titus for the challenges and opportunities of their work in the churches by writing the Pastoral Epistles, describing the qualifications, tasks, and conduct of Christian ministers.

But while Christians have long turned to the Pastoral Epistles for instruction in how to do the work of ministry, Paul's other letters have not typically been read with the same expectation. On first consideration this is unsurprising, as the Pastoral Epistles are decidedly oriented to the topic of ministry. Their very name suggests that pastors are going to find helpful direction and encouragement on their pages. Moreover, Paul's other letters might be neglected for instruction in this topic because the apostle is typically seen to fill the role of a missionary and itinerant church planter. He is not usually thought of as a pastor in the sense of the term that is familiar to us, that is, one who ministers to the spiritual needs of a local congregation on a regular basis.

Yet even a passing glance at Paul's ministry reveals that he was more than an evangelist and theologian, he was also a pastor. From the New Testament accounts we can see that he was regularly involved in the ongoing spiritual care of the Christians to whom he had first preached the gospel. In fact, Paul's pastoral work among the various congregations of the early decades of the church cannot be isolated from his other labors of gospel leadership and evangelism. For him the two activities went hand in hand: telling people about Christ, and then helping believers to grow in Christ.

How did Paul carry out his pastoral activities? He did so in a variety of ways, such as through visiting the churches personally and sending them his authorized representatives. But it seems that Paul's pastoring was conducted particularly through the letters he sent to various churches when he was unable to visit them. His letters provide not only an intimate look into the theological and ethical challenges faced by the early churches, but also into the way Paul sought to guide and exhort the congregations from a distance. It is a reasonable expectation, then, that through studying not just the Pastoral Epistles but the rest of Paul's letters, we can gain insight into the work of ministry as carried out by the apostle.

This brings us to 2 Corinthians. Even a cursory reading reveals its exceptionally personal and emotionally intense character among the letters of Paul. It offers an intriguing window into the apostle's relationship with one of the congregations he founded, the church at Corinth. Paul and the Corinthians apparently had a relationship of mutual affection, but one that also suffered times of strain and stress. In 2 Corinthians he alternates between pleading with them, warning them, teaching, rebuking, and reassuring them. For a variety of reasons that we will consider shortly, the Corinthians doubted Paul's dedication to them as a congregation. Besides this distrust, they favored other church leaders whose appearances were more impressive, whose oratory was more skillful, and who spoke more freely about their dramatic religious experiences.

Because of these criticisms and comparisons, Paul defends the way he has treated the Corinthians and has carried out his ministry among them. In this letter he provides a pointed apology for his character and conduct. At the same time, 2 Corinthians illustrates Paul's abiding devotion to this congregation. Despite the difficulties that are currently affecting their relationship, he instructs, warns, encourages, and commends the Corinthians, consistently expressing his delight in these believers and his great love for them in Christ. It is his Christ-shaped view of the Corinthians as their pastor that Paul wants the members of the congregation to understand and appreciate.

As we look at 2 Corinthians in coming chapters, we will examine how he expresses the character of his pastoral relationship with this congregation. We will give attention to those places where Paul speaks personally and directly to his readers by describing his holy privileges and weighty obligations as a pastor. Using a number of striking motifs and images, Paul endeavors to reveal the depths of his concern and affection for the Corinthians as their minister. It is Paul's considered view of his relationship with the Corinthians that will provide valuable aspects of a model for contemporary Christian ministry.

Of course, the social, cultural, and ecclesiastical situation has changed substantially from Paul's time to our own. We need to be cautioned against making illegitimate correlations between the practice of ministry in the first century and that in the twenty-first. Relating this to our study of 2 Corinthians and its portrayal of Paul's relationship with the congregation of Corinth, we note that any relationship is inevitably shaped by one's culture. Today there are different expectations and boundaries for personal relationships than were considered acceptable in the time of the apostle Paul. This means that the character of the involvement between a pastor and his congregation today can be expected to have changed to some degree.

Compounding this difficulty is Paul's distinctive position within the history of the Christian church. Paul was an apostle, and as such he possessed a unique ecclesiastical office that no longer functions today. And while some of Paul's peers (such as Timothy and Titus) held leadership positions in the early churches, ministry in Christian congregations at Paul's time was at best organized only at a rudimentary level. When Paul was involved in pastoring the Corinthians, there was not yet a developed structure of church authority to regulate or inform his actions. This meant that Paul was free to exercise the responsibilities and privileges of his position as he saw appropriate in the given circumstances, a freedom that is largely unavailable to pastors today—and probably for good reason!

The character of 2 Corinthians as a letter written at a specific occasion also warns against making simplistic application to the present time. Paul's letter is primarily a personal defense, with the legitimacy of his apostolic ministry being one of its chief concerns. This apologetic purpose casts the entire letter into a certain light. When reading and studying this remarkably personal epistle, we should be clear that Paul's primary intent was not to impart helpful instruction for those Christian leaders who might read the letter in later years. Consequently, we will see that many of the lessons that can be learned from 2 Corinthians need to be drawn indirectly. All of this means that we should exercise a measure of caution as we seek useful principles and guidelines from this letter.

While not every feature of Paul's relationship with the Corinthians can be applied to contemporary ministry, key elements remain relevant. Importantly, the letter itself suggests a basic continuity between Paul's relationship with the Corinthians and the modern-day pastor's relationship with a congregation. Despite Paul's unique historical role as an apostle, he consistently speaks not only of his own labors, but also about the labors of other servants of God in the church. While Paul is expounding on things that were true for his relationship with the Corinthians, it is clear that he is also writing about what he believes should be true of all those who have the privilege of ministering to Christ's people.

Though his focus is strongly apologetic, in this letter Paul still intends to teach a broader lesson for those who hold positions of Christian leadership. His rivals in Corinth would obviously not measure up to the high ministerial standard that he sets, which Paul eagerly wants this congregation to recognize. But the implication is that all true servants of Christ will conduct ministry in a way that is broadly similar to the apostle. Today, Christian pastors work with the same New Testament gospel of Jesus Christ, doing so in service of the same God and empowered by the same Holy Spirit. We can conclude that it is fitting that Christian ministry is still marked by the same patterns once demonstrated by Paul.

Finally, despite his high stature in the history of the church, in 2 Corinthians Paul reminds us that he struggled like any other human being. It is apparent that he had his own fears and burdens, and that he wrestled with personal weakness and inadequacy in carrying out his work. It is this most realistic picture of ministry that commends the apostle as an example for contemporary pastors, who all surely grapple at times with feelings of insufficiency and a sense of uncertainty as they work in Christ's church. It remains important that those who are involved in the work of pastoral ministry have good models to imitate and exemplars by which to be taught. And Pastor Paul stands as an excellent candidate for teaching such lessons.

In the coming chapters, we will take a closer look at the pressurized situation in first-century Corinth, the cultural challenges that Paul faced when ministering there, and how the challenges for pastors today are different yet comparable (chapter 1). We will then consider Paul's conception of ministerial identity and what he saw as his task in the church, before beginning to draw lines of comparison to ministerial identity and labors today (chapter 2). From there we will move on to examine one of Paul's principal metaphors for pastoring in 2 Corinthians: the notion of a pastor as father to his congregation (chapter 3). A central area of dispute between Paul and the Corinthians concerned his preaching, so we will explore how Paul portrays the preacher's task and message (chapter 4). This letter makes clear that Paul was facing a barrage of criticism, and his measured response to the Corinthians' reproaches and disparagements is instructive for every Christian pastor today (chapter 5). Paul must also respond to suspicions or complaints about the way in which he handled the matter of the Corinthians' financial support, another interaction that has contemporary relevance (chapter 6). From the first to the final chapter of 2 Corinthians, Paul speaks about his sufferings in ministry; far from downplaying this aspect of his work, he insists that hardship will be integral to the labors of any servant of Christ (chapter 7). In all his ministering among the occasionally recalcitrant and aloof Corinthians, Paul reveals that this letter was driven by a clear sense of pastoral purpose, earnestly desiring to see their faith grow into maturity and toward perfection at Christ's return (chapter 8). We will round off our exploration of 2 Corinthians with a closing reflection on the place of seeking fruits from our pastoral ministry while seeking grace from God even more. For it is only through God's mighty strength and with Christ's gospel that weak pastors will ever be effective.

CHAPTER 1

SERVING UNDER PRESSURE

For if I make you sorrowful, then who is he who makes me glad but the one who is made sorrowful by me?
—2 CORINTHIANS 2:2

It is not easy being a pastor. While the pastors gathered in a local ministerial group will probably find any number of issues to debate passionately—worship styles, infant or adult baptism, reliable Bible translations—with this statement surely all will agree with a solemn nodding of the head: it's not easy being a pastor. Even at the very best of times, when there is a spirit of peace in the congregation and the preaching is being well-received, when the pastoral workload is not too onerous and most of the youth seem to be moving in the right direction, it is not easy. Because even then, there can remain troubling feelings of inadequacy, when a pastor knows that he should do more and do it better. The work of being a pastor is often attended by a multitude of daily challenges, stresses, and niggling concerns. For instance, there are still those church members who rarely return pastoral phone calls or friendly texts, and the people on the far side of the auditorium who generally do not seem interested in your well-crafted and Christ-centered sermons each Sunday. And as in all of life, there are moods in ministry. Within the same span of seven days a pastor can go from having a joyful sense of strength and near invincibility—like that which can come after a particularly good

Sunday on the pulpit—to dark feelings of self-doubt, anxiety, and uselessness—like those which can arise after a couple of particularly difficult pastoral visits. Even when stress levels are low, there can remain the nagging forebodings of a looming burnout.

How much more difficult preaching and pastoral work can be when they are done in a pressurized atmosphere! Sometimes a congregation is bitterly divided in a dispute over a fine theological point, or over some local practice or policy. People are making their cases, taking sides, and are keen to see where the pastor stands. Sometimes there is the swelling influence of an unbiblical worldview or philosophy, one that is having a marked impact on how the members view their faith or the life of the church, and the pastor needs to respond. At other times, a pastor might face direct challenges to his own ministry. He might be unjustly accused of some wrongdoing, or his progressive (or regressive!) views might be perceived as a threat by some faction in the congregation. Or perhaps the pastoral performance standards in a congregation are so fluid that they are unachievable.

In such situations, a pastor can begin to fear that his ability to work in the congregation is being seriously hindered by the unrest, pressures, and criticisms. Even more seriously, the pastor might fear that some congregants have begun to weaken in their commitment to the true gospel. And if the gospel is thrown out, what is left? For a host of reasons, the hard task of pastoring can become even harder, and a minister and his congregation can be left wondering how the church can possibly move forward together in Christ. As we explore 2 Corinthians, we will see that the pressures on a pastor were all too familiar to Paul as he ministered to this congregation.

Flashback to First-Century Corinth

Reading 2 Corinthians is like eavesdropping while a stranger is talking on his phone next to you on the bus or in the grocery store. You are really curious to know what he is talking about, but you hear only one side of the conversation. In this letter we are allowed to hear one side of the conversation between Paul and this church, and it is a conversation about some intensely personal things, such as the history of their relationship, how they have been treating each other lately, and what they can reasonably expect from each other. And at times the conversation gets heated with emotion.

Before looking at the difficulties that Paul encountered in his long and complicated relationship with the Corinthians, let us consider who these people were and the backstory of Paul's connection with them. It was sometime around AD 51 that the apostle Paul, while on his second missionary journey, arrived in the city of Corinth. When he arrived, what kind of city did he find? Corinth was a city with a checkered past. From before the fifth century BC, it had thrived as a Greek city-state. Then, as the principal city of the Achaean League, it was completely destroyed by Roman legions in 146 BC after a conflict with the imperial capital. For about one hundred years the site of the ruined Corinth lay untouched, until the city was refounded by a decree of Julius Caesar in 44 BC. There were good reasons that Caesar saw fit to reestablish the city. First, its location on the isthmus between Peloponnesus and mainland Greece meant that Corinth had a strategic position, commercially and militarily. Second, the plan was to repopulate Corinth with Roman freedmen, the sort of folk who were not always welcome in the more established imperial cities.

On account of its excellent location, the city of Corinth was quickly thriving once again. A large segment of the population was employed as artisans and craftsmen, and they soon began to produce significant wealth. Many migrants came to the city with their gods, with the result that before long Corinth had numerous sacred places that were devoted to the deities of the Greco-Roman pantheon. But a strong economy and an enthusiastic paganism were the same ingredients that made it a city of rampant immorality. Corinth had a culture of greed and competition, with many wild parties and few moral inhibitions. Already the old Corinth had a reputation for sexual vices, and Corinth 2.0 proved little different. If you had to compare first-century Corinth with some modern-day city, you might think of Las Vegas, Nevada, USA. Corinth was the "Sin City" of the Roman Empire.

The character of Corinth as a freshly reestablished and deliberately egalitarian city had a tangible impact on its social structures. Without a deep-rooted aristocracy, the Corinthian population enjoyed the real possibility of upward mobility. This was a place where almost anyone could get ahead, and certainly more than a few Corinthians had the goal of social progression. However, while its climate was favorable for the socially ambitious, Corinth remained a city that preserved the basic Roman cultural values. New city or not, in Corinth it remained true that an individual's status was still closely tied to the same host of external factors that were so valued in other parts of the empire: employment, education, wealth, religion, family, and ethnicity. The desire to conform to these social standards led many Corinthians to project outward prestige and to seek honor in any possible way. They did so through choosing and arranging suitable marriage partners, aggressively accumulating wealth, and cultivating good social connections. A proverb from the Roman poet Horace illustrated the general character of first-century Corinth: "Not for everyone is the voyage to Corinth." To survive in this town you needed to be strong, and to get ahead you had to be ruthless.

The Troubled Congregation

Into this complex and demanding social setting Paul entered, and at Corinth he soon founded a Christian congregation. Now, it has always been hard—even impossible—for Christians not to be affected by the cultures that daily surround them. Both of Paul's letters to the Corinthians bear undeniable witness to the fact that the Corinthian milieu dramatically shaped the church in that place. This context has a significant impact on the issues that arose in Paul's pastoral care for these believers.

Among New Testament scholars there is a long-standing debate about the precise social class of the Corinthian Christians. The makeup of the Corinthian church—and that of other Christian congregations from this early period—has usually been understood to be largely lower class, those who were materially poor and socially debased. Paul's own words have been used in support of this view, for in 1 Corinthians he writes, "God has chosen the foolish things of the world to put to shame the wise, and God has chosen the weak things of the world to put to shame the things which are mighty; and the base things of the world and the things which are despised God has chosen, and the things which are not, to bring to nothing the things that are" (1:27–28).

To put it another way, there were probably not many in the church on the who's who list of first-century Corinth.

Nonetheless, it is also likely that there were some members of the higher classes in the Corinthian church alongside the many slaves and freedmen. As in other early Christian churches, this congregation probably reflected a cross section of urban society, with people from varied social layers, ranging from the lower-class majority to a few upper-class church members. As we will see in a later chapter, it was almost certainly members of a socially pretentious group in Corinth who came under the sway of the new spiritual leaders. These leaders' influence in the congregation gave rise to the pressurized situation that caused such grief for Paul during his times of absence from Corinth.

Already when he wrote his first letter to the Corinthians, Paul was concerned about a nasty spirit of division that was simmering in the new congregation. People were taking sides and favoring one leader over another: "For it has been declared to me concerning you, my brethren, by those of Chloe's household, that there are contentions among you. Now I say this, that each of you says, 'I am of Paul,' or 'I am of Apollos,' or 'I am of Cephas,' or 'I am of Christ'" (1 Cor. 1:11–12; cf. 11:18–22). Having heard this bad report, Paul condemns such jealousy and strife as completely inappropriate for those who should no longer live according to the sinful nature but according to the Holy Spirit (3:3–4). Yet in Corinth this acrimony seems to have persisted—even worsened—and it was likely a factor in the conflict lying behind Paul's pained words throughout 2 Corinthians.

Paul's Strenuous Ministering

The conversation unfolding in 2 Corinthians is one that had started years before. As mentioned, Paul visited this city while on his second missionary journey. Luke reports in Acts 18:11 that the apostle spent eighteen months teaching and ministering in Corinth, which is a fairly long period compared to his work in other places. Different reasons for this lengthy stay have been suggested. Some scholars say that because of its unique geography, Corinth was an ideal location from which the gospel could be spread throughout the region. Others suggest that because of its strong economy, Corinth afforded Paul the opportunity to practice his trade as a tentmaker and to maintain financial independence, the model of ministry support that he preferred. It has also been pointed out that because of its large population of slaves and freedmen—people with less of a need or opportunity to conform to the expectations of respectable society—Corinth's residents might have been more disposed to associate with the "new" religion that Paul was promoting.

Whatever the reason for Paul's lengthy stay in Corinth initially, these eighteen months were not sufficient to shape the congregation for continuing well in the faith. This is clear from the various letters that Paul wrote to them in later years, in addition to sending them personal delegates and making further visits to Corinth himself. After Paul's first departure from Corinth, he wrote a letter that was apparently meant to address some of the congregation's issues around sexual ethics (1 Cor. 5:9). This is a letter that is no longer in existence. He followed up this first letter with a second, which is the canonical letter of 1 Corinthians. From 1 Corinthians we learn about the numerous problems that were disturbing this congregation, including internal division, sexual immorality, and false teaching. In his letter Paul advises them that he intends to return to Corinth later (16:5–8). Meanwhile, however, he has dispatched Timothy in order to visit and instruct the congregation (4:17).

After the letter of 1 Corinthians was received, there seems to have been a measure of progress in the congregation. However, things soon began to decline sharply. When Timothy visited Corinth, he discovered that some individuals had infiltrated the congregation and turned a significant portion of the people against Paul. It appears that these opponents were not originally part of the congregation but entered later and were able to rise to positions of leadership and influence. As becomes clear from Paul's impassioned words in 2 Corinthians, these rival leaders' teaching has thoroughly confused the congregation's view of Christian ministry. It is nothing less than a clash of ideologies, for Paul's conception of a weak and suffering ministry was shaped by the gospel of the crucified Christ, while their view was shaped by worldly considerations of power and appearance.

In response to Timothy's troubling report about what is transpiring in Corinth, Paul interrupts his work in Asia Minor in order to make a second visit to the congregation. We do not know exactly what unfolded when he visited, but the pastor-congregation interactions apparently ended in disaster (2 Cor. 2:1–2). In the aftermath of this visit, Paul sent Titus to the Corinthians, carrying a tearful letter of admonition (2:4). This letter has also likely been lost, though some scholars have tried to identify it with 1 Corinthians or with portions of 2 Corinthians 10–13. Paul reports that the delay of Titus in returning from Corinth caused him no small anxiety (2 Cor. 2:12–13), but eventually Titus rejoined Paul in Macedonia when he had a more positive report to share about the condition of the congregation.

It is when Paul has just heard this encouraging news about the congregation that he writes 2 Corinthians. He then sends Titus back to Corinth in order to consolidate the recent gains and also to do further pastoral work in the congregation (8:6, 16–24). Paul shares with them that he himself plans to visit the Corinthians—this will now be the third time (12:14)—a visit he seems to have accomplished later while traveling to Jerusalem (Rom. 15:24–29).

Reviewing all this contact, it is clear that the believers in Corinth were the object of Paul's pastoral attention over a substantial length of time and with a high degree of intensity. As will be seen in coming chapters, it is Paul's devotion to the church of Corinth—even in troubled circumstances, and with limited pastoral opportunities—that stands as an inspiring example for pastors today. When a pastor has the conviction that his congregation's growth in Christ is of paramount importance, he will be strenuous in ministering to them and devoted in caring for them. And as Paul's ministry illustrates, a vigorous ministry in a particular place requires the use of a wide range of pastoral tools. For Paul this included congregational visits, sermons and teaching, personal delegates, and impassioned letters, while for us the tools will be such things as pastoral visits, sermons and teaching, phone calls, text messages, and more.

Pastoring Then and Now

Paul's difficulty in conducting ministry in a thoroughly pagan and pressurized environment is an experience that is shared by many contemporary pastors. While the days of the Roman Empire and first-century Corinth are long gone, we should not exaggerate the cultural contrasts between Paul's day and ours. Indeed, the first-century Corinthian milieu is not so far removed from today's culture. We might not live in ancient Corinth or in modern Las Vegas, but sin's insidious effects on the church and its members are not new. For instance, as there was in Corinth, in our society there is still an obsession with prestige and recognition, together with contempt for those who do not have any notable status. Similarly, the tendency to divide along party lines and to erect barriers against the other side is a sad and enduring inclination of the human heart.

Comparing Corinth to your own town or city will reveal many differences of detail, but there is an essential similarity in the general circumstances of believers being surrounded by a dominant non-Christian culture. Whenever Christian truth is being preached and taught in an environment where the social standards and values are non-Christian, pastors are going to be challenged in their work of leading and caring for the church. And so church leaders will do well to consider carefully the ways in which Paul responded to cultural influences in order to minister faithfully and effectively to the Corinthians.

As he addresses the Corinthians in his letter, Paul uses language that is at times strong and pointed. Because of their willingness to conform to godless culture, he can be sarcastic and almost harsh with the congregation (see, e.g., 2 Cor. 11:19). Yet from the very first words of 2 Corinthians, it is clear that he considers these believers to be the blessed recipients of God's saving grace in Christ Jesus (1:2). Later in the letter, Paul finds reason to delight in the work that God is doing in this church, even among the brothers and sisters who have cruelly disparaged his ministry. This persistently loving approach was surely informed by Paul's awareness of his own dependence on God's mercy in Christ. He needed the Father's forgiveness of sins just as much as the Corinthians, and he daily needed Christ's empowering grace just as much as the Corinthians (12:9).

This deep humility before God is fundamental for pastoral practice even when working in a church environment that is pressurized and frustrating. A wise elder once shared with me that before going to a congregational member's home for a pastoral visit, he would take a few moments to remind himself about his own sin, how on that particular day he had invariably failed to love God and his neighbor. On the visit he did not want to share Scripture, ask probing questions, or dispense advice from a position of superiority, but rather to do so from a deliberate posture of humility, knowing that as an elder he, too, lived by the all-sufficient grace of God in Christ. Considering oneself to be graciously forgiven in Christ rightly humbles a person when experiencing the friction and discomfort of coming into contact with other people's rough edges. The reality is that ministry is always going to be hard, and there will always be pressures from within and without. Accepting this fact allows a pastor to approach his work not only with a sense of level-headedness, but with a humble dependence on Christ who has given His servants a rich gospel, a high purpose, and abundant strength. In the next chapter we will consider further how Paul's identity—and every pastor's identity—is shaped by God's grace toward us in His Son.

CHAPTER 2

BUILDING A
MINISTERIAL IDENTITY

*For we do not preach ourselves, but Christ Jesus the Lord, and
ourselves your bondservants for Jesus' sake.*

—2 CORINTHIANS 4:5

If you are fortunate enough to have a job, then you probably also
have a job description. A job description outlines what is expected
of a person in a position of employment: "When at work, these are
your duties, the various tasks that you are responsible for. Here are
the requirements that you need to meet." A job description is helpful in providing direction and focus for your work, and hopefully in
preventing you from becoming overloaded with additional duties.
Whatever your task, whether a stay-at-home mom, an employee in
a fast-food restaurant, a carpenter's assistant, or an accountant, it is
beneficial to have a clear idea of what the expectations are for your
daily work.

It is little different for a Christian pastor, yet this is an occupation
that has often been saddled with a job description that is unhelp-
fully vague and ill-defined—if there is a job description at all! Even
when a pastor's basic duties are outlined in a book of church order
or mentioned during an ordination service, there can remain an
impenetrable aura of mystery around what a pastor does. In the past,
children in my congregations have asked me in all seriousness, "So,

what do you *do* all week?" They saw me at church for a couple hours every Sunday, but wondered how I filled the other six days.

These are important questions for a pastor to reflect on: What ministerial activities should have my attention? How do I set the priorities for my work? What am I really supposed to be doing? For, to be sure, a pastor who is very busy every day is not necessarily a pastor who is working effectively or intentionally. Without a firm sense of his duties, a pastor could waste a lot of time on frivolous or peripheral activities, and he could neglect the work that is necessary for the congregation's spiritual well-being. In the same way, it is helpful for a congregation to be clear on just what their pastor is supposed to be doing among them from week to week.

It is precisely this issue that Paul addresses in 2 Corinthians. He is writing this letter as the "part-time pastor" or adjunct minister of the church at Corinth. In the previous chapter we saw that having first preached the gospel to the Corinthians, Paul continued to be involved with these believers through periodic visits and letters. Paul and this congregation once enjoyed times of mutual blessing when he labored among them and they gladly received his preaching and pastoring. But such happy days were a fading memory, for the Corinthians had changed their expectations for him and his ministry while comparing him with ministers who were seemingly more capable. Some people in the church were now concluding that Paul was not up to the task. In this letter he defends himself against their allegations and criticisms, while also teaching them about the true job description of a gospel minister.

Paul's Ministerial Identity

In all his ministerial labors, Paul was moved by the desire to perform devoted service for the spiritual benefit of Christ's people. This stood in marked contrast to his rivals in Corinth, who were embraced by the congregation despite their domineering attitude and heavy-handed actions. Paul's bewilderment at this turn of events is evident: "For you put up with it if one brings you into bondage, if one devours you, if one takes from you, if one exalts himself, if one strikes you on the face" (2 Cor. 11:20). His opponents had shown that it was possible to do outwardly impressive ministerial work while lacking any real concern for the congregation. Such domineering was not Paul's modus operandi. Rather, he cherishes the position of being a servant to the Corinthians, not their authoritarian ruler. Although certain aspects of Paul's character (e.g., his meekness) or his conduct (e.g., his self-funding) were offensive and embarrassing to the socially conscious Corinthians, he does not deny or minimize these elements of his ministry. Instead, he champions them as indicative of his devotion to the church! Paul's identity as a humble servant is grounded in the cross of Christ, where God's power worked so effectively through great weakness (13:4).

While it is largely Paul's reaction to his opponents that shapes this letter, he still has a positive purpose. He is trying to persuade the Corinthians to take a view of ministry that is consistent with the true message of the cross of Christ. He also seeks to relieve any uncertainty about himself as an apostle so that their faith does not suffer. Indeed, Paul defends himself in order to strengthen the congregation's confidence in him as Christ's servant, while simultaneously urging them not to abandon the true gospel they received through his ministry. He desires that the Corinthians will come to appreciate his pastoral view of them: "Now I trust you will understand, even to the end (as also you have understood us in part), that we are your boast as you also are ours, in the day of the Lord Jesus" (1:13–14).

As Paul explains the nature of his ministry to the Corinthians, he employs a few key terms that collectively describe his identity. He sees himself as an apostle commissioned by Christ, as an ambassador of God, and as a slave of the churches for Jesus's sake. Each of these terms conveys a different aspect of his work, and together they provide insight into Paul's understanding of his pastoral labors among the congregations that he established. At the same time, each of these terms can offer clarifying instruction and heartening encouragement to pastors who are busy working in Christ's church today.

Apostle

Throughout his many letters to the churches, it is clear that Paul sees apostleship as a central aspect of his ministerial identity. Already in the first letter to the Corinthians, he emphasized this position when he introduced himself: "Paul, called to be an apostle of Jesus Christ through the will of God" (1 Cor. 1:1). In the opening verse of this second letter, too, he reminds the Corinthians of his God-given position, identifying himself as "Paul, an apostle of Jesus Christ by the will of God" (2 Cor. 1:1). In the New Testament, the apostles were those whom Christ first commissioned to establish the church through making disciples of all nations (Matt. 28:19–20). Having accompanied Jesus during His three years of ministry, the apostles were able to provide a solid foundation of eyewitness testimony to His life, death, and resurrection (Acts 1:21).

Now, Paul's own background as an apostle was decidedly different from that of the original twelve apostles, for Paul had not participated in the events of Jesus's ministry. Rather, in the early days of the Christian church he had actively opposed Christ and those who preached His message (Acts 7:58; 8:1–3). But the Lord was merciful, revealing Himself to Paul and calling him to service. The apostle gratefully recounts this divine intervention in his first letter to the Corinthians: "Last of all He was seen by me also, as by one born out of due time. For I am the least of the apostles, who am not worthy to be called an apostle, because I persecuted the church of God" (1 Cor. 15:8–9). Jesus graciously entrusted His message of salvation to Paul, who accepted it as his vocation to preach Christ's gospel in the many places of the world where it had not yet been preached (Rom. 15:20; Gal. 1:15–16).

We have already seen how Paul's apostolic ministry was the target of his opponents' attacks. Through their belittling of his personal character and ministerial conduct, they ravaged his status as an apostle and elevated themselves as the legitimate apostles and leaders in the Corinthian congregation. The nature of this sharp antagonism makes Paul's response in 2 Corinthians surprising, for unlike other letters where he addressed questions about his legitimacy as an apostle (e.g., Galatians), here Paul does not link his position to his encounter with the risen Christ. He certainly does in 1 Corinthians 9:1: "Am I not an apostle? Am I not free? Have I not seen Jesus Christ our Lord? Are you not my work in the Lord?" But in 2 Corinthians, where one might have expected Paul to make another appeal to his apostolic authority in order to squelch criticism or to command submission, he does not. He will not blast them with an apostolic injunction, nor appeal to the accomplishments that would confirm his superiority as a Christian leader. Only toward the end of 2 Corinthians does he reluctantly allude to the "visions and revelations of the Lord" that he received (12:1). And almost in passing, he mentions that he, too, had displayed the signs and works of an apostle (12:12). Far more emphatically throughout the letter he points to his sufferings in union with Christ. It is indeed hardships that commend his authority as an apostle (cf. 1 Cor. 4:9). As we will see in a later chapter, Paul considers that his ministry only has power through its conformity to Christ's example of suffering service at the cross.

Even when he tells the Corinthians that he is speaking with his God-given authority (2 Cor. 10:8; 13:10), he is careful to highlight his bond with the glorified Christ. Above all, it was his connection to Jesus that Paul wants his churches to benefit from spiritually. As he insists in 2 Corinthians 1:24, "Not that we have dominion over your faith, but are fellow workers for your joy; for by faith you stand." Even though he is gifted and greatly accomplished as an apostle— and even though he has been personally appointed by Christ—Paul does not set himself in an imperious position above the people to whom he is ministering. More than anything, he wants to use his position in order to strengthen their grip on the gospel.

This aim helps us understand Paul's fatherly pleading to his children in 2 Corinthians 6:13: "Now in return for the same (I speak as to children), you also be open." In the next chapter we will consider the meaning of this poignant declaration more closely, but for now let us note how it clearly expresses Paul's view of his pastoral relationship with this church. Because he has been instrumental as an apostle in preaching the gospel and bringing them to faith, he desires that the Corinthians respond to him in an honest and humble way. It is particularly in order to help them spiritually that he desires the Corinthians' renewed allegiance and devotion.

Paul's refusal to brandish his apostolic authority in a domineering manner over the Corinthians offers a helpful example for those who are busy with caring for Christ's church today. In God's providence, a pastor or church leader has been given a position of authority and influence. Even though being a pastor is a holy work done for the spiritual benefit of Christ's believers, there is an insidious temptation to use this position for personal gain. It does not take long for a minister to realize that he could flaunt his status in the congregation to his own benefit and glory. Because a pastor is generally held in high esteem by his church, it can become an alluring possibility to him that he can sway people with an appeal to his academic training, his various accomplishments, and his ecclesiastical office: "I know more than you, I have done more than you, and I have a higher position than you—so you ought to listen to me." But a pastor who is tempted by a desire for fawning approval and awestruck praise should remember the apostle Paul in 2 Corinthians, who was reluctant to tout his privileged position. Instead, he was eager to affirm his identity as a weak and suffering servant of the church for Jesus's sake. Unlike Paul, a pastor is not an apostle, but a pastor has nevertheless received his high position from Christ. And so he should conduct himself in this position in a Christlike way, demonstrating humility and performing loyal service for the good of the Lord's people.

Ambassador
A second essential aspect of Paul's pastoral identity is that he is an ambassador for Christ. He writes in 2 Corinthians 5:19–20, "God was in Christ reconciling the world to Himself, not imputing their trespasses to them, and has committed to us the word of reconciliation. Now then, we are ambassadors for Christ, as though God were pleading through us: we implore you on Christ's behalf, be reconciled to God." The concept of an ambassador was well known in the

first century world. In Paul's time, ambassadors had a somewhat different task than they have today. In today's geopolitical context, ambassadors are sent to the capital of a particular country on a long-term basis. For example, Canada's ambassador to the United States will usually reside in Washington, DC, for several years so that he or she can make known the official Canadian positions and interests on all kinds of important matters. By contrast, ambassadors in the first century were sent to other countries according to need. For instance, if a conflict between Rome and a small region in the backwaters of the empire was threatening to erupt in violence, an ambassador would step in to assist. Typically, such an ambassador would be hired by those who had the most to lose, those in the more vulnerable position, economically or militarily. In our scenario, the backwaters region would send an ambassador to the capital city in order to try to bring about a good resolution of the problem.

In what sense are sinners in need of an ambassador? God has supreme authority in this universe, for He has created all things, governs all things, and expects full obedience from all of His creatures. Yet there is a sharp conflict between God and His human subjects, for by our sin we have rejected His claim on us. God could justly crush our rebellion, but He unexpectedly provides an ambassador in order to make peace. Notice that it is not the belligerent frontier people or the poor peasants who send a petition to the mighty king and plead for his mercy. The gospel of Christ turns everything upside down, for it is God who graciously reaches out to the people who chose to be alienated from Him! It is the blameless king, the very one who has been offended, who chooses to send an ambassador to bring about reconciliation and peace. This is the glory of God, who breaks all the patterns and precedents of human relationships by "pleading...be reconciled to God" (5:20).

God pleads that sinners accept His plan for peace so that we might live and not die. God makes this restoration possible through His only Son, who is the original Ambassador and who personally carried the guilt of the rebels. And now Christ employs human servants in order to bring His message of peace to all the world; as Paul writes in 2 Corinthians 5:18, "Now all things are of God, who has reconciled us to Himself through Jesus Christ, and has given us the ministry of reconciliation." Serving as an ambassador for Christ, Paul was entrusted with a word from his royal Master, for God through him was making His gracious appeal to sinners (cf. Eph. 6:19–20).

Similar to today, an ambassador in the first-century world held a prestigious position. But Paul, as the envoy of Christ, was not looking for special treatment—the Corinthians could keep the red carpet rolled up. They had been criticizing him, laughing at his letters, and making fun of the way he spoke. Paul could endure all this as long as they accepted his message. In his ambassadorial role, he pleads with them "on Christ's behalf" (2 Cor. 5:20). God had given up far too much—even His one and only Son—to allow the Corinthians to fall back into darkness. Paul's message to them was most consequential, even a matter of life and death. Would the Corinthians receive Paul for who he was and accept his words as a message from the Lord? Such was his urgent prayer.

This was how Paul saw his task, and this is how pastors can continue to see their task today. As ambassadors, pastors carry an appeal from Christ and God. They must never tire of saying to sinners, "Be reconciled to your Creator. Make sure that you are right with God through Christ His Son." Pastors come as representatives of the one whom God sent from heaven, emissaries of the one who brought peace through His precious blood. This remains the living center, the beating heart, and the firm foundation of whatever message a pastor brings. For instance, when visiting someone in his or her home or in a café, there is much that a pastor can talk about. Pastoral discussion can be wide-ranging, from personal devotions to financial stewardship, from caring for children to assisting elderly parents, from church life to our place in a post-Christian society. Even so, a pastor's message must never neglect Christ and the salvation that He accomplished, the reconciliation with God that He made possible. As ambassadors for Christ, pastors want everyone to be sure that they have peace with God. "How about you?" a pastor should ask. "How is your relationship with the Lord? Have you been reconciled to your creator through Christ? And how has this changed you? In what way has this peace changed your life?"

This message gives a true staying power to the pastoral task. In their work, pastors certainly feel at times like giving up on those who are hardened in sin, perhaps walking away from the stubborn and negative members of the congregation. But then they should meditate on how God has reached out with love, sending His well-beloved Son as ambassador and pleading with them and all sinners to return. In making this peace, ponder what Christ gave up: His own blood, His own life. The Father and the Son did not capitulate in the face of evil or hardship, and neither should pastors. This is what gave Paul the resolve to stay in his post as ambassador, even when the Corinthians suggested every reason to walk away. In fact, as much as he may have wanted to abandon this congregation, Paul was obliged to continue working: "For the love of Christ compels us, because we judge thus: that if One died for all, then all died" (5:14). Pastors should know how lost they themselves would be without Christ's love; as ambassadors, this is a message they have first received and accepted for themselves. Now they are compelled to pass it on—to keep preaching it and sharing it from house to house—because they have started to understand and experience how beautiful this message really is.

Slave

The notion of authority in his identity as an apostle and the sense of honor in his position as an ambassador of Christ are balanced in 2 Corinthians by Paul's reference to himself as a slave of the churches and of God. In an instructive passage, Paul writes, "For we do not preach ourselves, but Christ Jesus the Lord, and ourselves your bondservants for Jesus' sake" (4:5). The Greek term (*doulos*), translated "bondservant" in the New King James Version, is rendered more accurately as "slave." In the first century, a slave did not belong to himself but to someone else; he had given up authority over himself and subordinated his will entirely to the will of another person. The life of a slave was earmarked for labor that would be for the benefit of the master and his household. This was another key aspect in Paul's ministerial identity: he was a slave.

It is notable in 2 Corinthians 4:5 that Paul sees his servitude as performed for the congregation: we are "*your* bondservants for Jesus' sake." With this image of a bondservant he wants the Corinthians to recognize that his ministerial work for their sakes will be wide-ranging and dedicated. The believers' spiritual well-being was far more important than his own, for Paul's privilege was to carry forward the message of Christ for their benefit. As such, he is content to be debased in their eyes, as long as this does not detract from their acceptance of his message about Christ. Using a Greek term with a different root, *diakonoi* ("servants"), Paul had asked in his first letter, "What then is Apollos? What is Paul? Servants through whom you believed, as the Lord assigned to each" (1 Cor. 3:5 ESV). Through his committed labors, he desires that sinners would come to saving faith in Christ and bear the resultant fruits of faith.

As a slave of Jesus, Paul will diligently seek the advantage of the churches and not his own benefit. This is how he spoke of his ministry in his first letter, "Though I am free from all men, *I have made myself a servant to all*, that I might win the more" (1 Cor. 9:19). Since then, his opponents in Corinth had been making accusations about Paul's lack of devotion to the church, his shortage of love, and his harsh and high-handed dealings. But Paul wants the Corinthians to see that he is not seeking to bully them, but to serve them and build them up. Indeed, as a servant he would do anything for their spiritual strengthening. Paul would sacrifice, he would suffer, even die, as long as it served the Corinthians and helped them embrace the true gospel. As he says about his many ministerial sufferings in 2 Corinthians 4, "All things are for your sakes" (v. 15). Everything that he did was to serve the church.

A pastor today might hesitate at this aspect of ministerial identity. He wonders, Am I really required by Jesus to be a slave, here in the twenty-first century? Am I to be a free man, yet live as the servant of the congregation? This does not agree with our modern sensibilities. Putting "slave" into a pastor's job description is probably prohibited by the labor laws! So why should anyone be willing to serve like this? Notably, Paul says that he is the church's servant "for Jesus' sake" (2 Cor. 4:5). This is the challenging truth revealed in 2 Corinthians: being a servant is basic to a pastor's job description because this is exactly what Christ did. Though He was God Almighty, Christ "made Himself of no reputation, taking the form of a bondservant, and coming in the likeness of men" (Phil. 2:7). Christ esteemed others better than Himself and constantly looked not to His own interests but to the interests of others. This attitude of humble service took Jesus all the way to death on an accursed cross. Paul's injunction in Philippians 2:5—"Let this mind be in you which was also in Christ Jesus"—means that this will always be the character of true ministry and true Christian service, becoming like Christ in our commitment to others.

This identity teaches us that a true pastor is not akin to a tyrant wielding a Bible, exerting power over the people without love. He is also not a sanctified celebrity, hungry for the congregation's likes and recognition. Neither is he an ecclesiastical CEO, looking to be enriched and served by his underlings. If a pastor tries to please himself, he is forgetting whose servant he is. Indeed, a selfish pastor is actually subverting Christ's gospel through his attitude and actions. Likewise, if a pastor is trying primarily to please the congregation, or the board of elders who hired him, or a certain demographic within the church, then he forgets whose servant he is. On the contrary, a true pastor is a slave of Christ, a servant who has committed himself to the spiritual progress of the believers. A pastor must always approach his task with the attitude of putting others ahead of himself for Jesus's sake. A pastor should resolve to keep asking this single question throughout the varied duties of his ministry: What can I do to help? Serving in a Christlike spirit, he can ask this constantly of the people in his care: How can I help you in your grief? How can I help you in your trouble? How can I help you in your uncertainty? How can I teach you? How can I encourage you? Let me be of service, any way that I can. Let me pray with you and bring the Word of Christ to you. This is consistent with the model of ministry that is also sketched by the apostle and "fellow elder" Peter in his first letter: "Shepherd the flock of God which is among you, serving as overseers, not by compulsion but willingly, not for dishonest gain but eagerly; nor as being lords over those entrusted to you, but being examples to the flock" (1 Peter 5:2–3). Christ will surely use a willing and humble servant to accomplish much good in His church.

A Portrait of Ministry

Paul's portrait of ministry in 2 Corinthians gives profound insight into the work that he performed among the churches in the first century. At the same time, this portrayal provides important guidance regarding the character and emphasis of pastoral work today. Churches and pastors alike can be clear on the job description of a pastor by returning to the foundational documents of the church, the New Testament Scriptures. Writing as he does in a different time and culture, we cannot expect Paul to spell out every detail of contemporary ministry. But through Paul's portrait of ministerial identity, the Holy Spirit focuses attention on what is most important for pastors today:

- For whom is your daily work as pastor being done? If you have the conviction that it was Christ who called and sent you, are you laboring for Him?

- As you work, what is your ultimate desire for the congregation? Do you long to see people reconciled to God through faith in Christ Jesus?

- In what spirit are your labors in the church being carried out? Are you a humble and dedicated servant of the congregation for Jesus's sake?

CHAPTER 3

PASTORING LIKE A FATHER

*Now in return for the same (I speak
as to children), you also be open.*
—2 CORINTHIANS 6:13

When Paul wrote 2 Corinthians, he was an afflicted man seeking comfort—or he *had* been afflicted, and God comforted him. In the first chapter he says that the many hardships of ministry and the tensions with the Corinthians had caused him to feel "burdened beyond measure," as if he was carrying a load that was "above [his] strength" to carry (2 Cor. 1:8). But Paul testifies that in his acute need he has learned to rely on God, who is able to provide sure comfort and even to raise the dead (v. 9). And so he opens the letter with a thankful doxology: "Blessed be the God and Father of our Lord Jesus Christ, the Father of mercies and God of all comfort, who comforts us in all our tribulation" (vv. 3–4).

God the Father had shown mercy to Paul in his weakness and reassured him in his uncertainties. Perhaps Paul had been comforted through a remembrance of God's Old Testament promises or through a consoling message spoken directly by the Lord (see 12:9). In any case, the apostle experienced personally the goodness of God the Father—a comfort that Paul in turn was able to share with the Corinthians: "We may be able to comfort those who are in any trouble, with the comfort with which we ourselves are comforted by God" (1:4). It is his gratitude to God the Father through Christ that compels Paul to continue in the work of pastoring the church, and it is the example of the Father's comforting mercy and goodness that provides him with a fitting model for his ministry. In this chapter we will see how Paul aims to do the work of a fatherly pastor, as should every pastor who is privileged to serve the "Father of our Lord Jesus Christ."

A New Family

There is a variety of New Testament images for the work of a pastor or overseer. Perhaps best known is the metaphor of an elder as a shepherd who tends and feeds God's flock (see John 21:15–17; Acts 20:28–29; 1 Peter 5:1–4). In the Pastoral Epistles, Paul uses a household term to speak of the work of pastors, calling them a "vessel" who will be "sanctified and useful for the Master, prepared for every good work" (2 Tim. 2:21). It is striking that in 2 Corinthians—perhaps the most pastoral of the letters that he wrote to his scattered congregations— much of what Paul writes about his attitude toward the church can be unified under the image of a father. For instance, his words to them in 2 Corinthians 6:11–13 are most direct and personal, "O Corinthians! We have spoken openly to you, our heart is wide open. You are not restricted by us, but you are restricted by your own affections. Now in return for the same (I speak as to children), you also be open." In pleading for their affection, Paul reminds them that in a real sense he is their father, and that he desires an open and loving relationship, which will be to their benefit.

The image of a pastor as a parent—both father *and* mother—is found elsewhere in Paul's epistles. Writing to the Corinthians in his first letter, Paul asserts, "For though you might have ten thousand instructors in Christ, yet you do not have many fathers; for in Christ Jesus I have begotten you through the gospel" (1 Cor. 4:15). In Galatians, too, he uses parental imagery, but this time in a remarkably maternal sense: "My little children, for whom I labor in birth again until Christ is formed in you" (Gal. 4:19). To the Thessalonian believers, Paul portrays himself both as a tender mother—"we were gentle among you, just as a nursing mother cherishes her own children"

(1 Thess. 2:7)—and also as a loving and earnest father: "You know how we exhorted, and comforted, and charged every one of you, as a father does his own children, that you would walk worthy of God who calls you into His own kingdom and glory" (vv. 11–12). Paul clearly saw the image of a parent as a powerful metaphor for his ongoing work of ministry among the churches.

This parent-child language can first be seen in connection with the family terminology that is characteristic of not just the Pauline Epistles but every New Testament letter. Central to New Testament theology is the truth that all believers constitute a new family in Christ under God the Father through the indwelling Holy Spirit (see, e.g., John 1:12–13; Rom. 8:14–17; Gal. 4:4–7). Formerly they were strangers to each other—particularly if they lived on opposite sides of the dividing wall between Jew and Gentile—but now Paul and his converts enjoy the intimate ties that are produced by a shared faith in Christ. Within these bonds, the apostle often addresses the members of his churches as "brothers and sisters," a phrase that he employs in his epistles more than sixty times.

In light of this frequency, it is notable that in an epistle as lengthy as 2 Corinthians, the readers are addressed as "brothers and sisters" just three times. The infrequency of sibling language in this letter, as well as the regular occurrence of paternal language, may be due to how the relationship between Paul and the Corinthians has been strained. The equality implicit in the language of "brothers and sisters" has been supplanted by the use of "father," a term suggestive of not only authority but also affection and nurture. It probably also served as a subtle reminder to the Corinthians that God had used Paul to bring them to faith (cf. 1 Cor. 4:15); he is the father by whom this congregation has been spiritually begotten. Over against the competing claims of Paul's opponents, the Corinthians needed to reflect on how Paul had a contributing role in their status as Christians, even from the moment of their conversion. Consequently, they should gladly accept his ongoing guidance, admonition, and affection.

The Task of Fathers

In the Old Testament, the role and position of a father carried a marked sense of authority. Fathers were expected to impart instruction to their children; for instance, in Proverbs 1:8 Solomon exhorts, "My son, hear the instruction of your father, and do not forsake the law of your mother." And again in Proverbs 4:1, "Hear, my children, the instruction of a father, and give attention to know understanding" (cf. 6:20). In Jewish culture, children were taught the obligation to honor their parents, particularly their fathers (Ex. 20:12; Prov. 13:1; 15:5; 29:15). A faithful father would also correct and discipline his son if he was straying from God's way: "He who spares his rod hates his son, but he who loves him disciplines him promptly" (Prov. 13:24). Thus, in the Old Testament someone who provided good and meaningful instruction to a younger person might also be called "father," even if they had no biological connection (see, e.g., 2 Kings 2:12).

Within the Greco-Roman world, the father had a similarly prominent social role. The *paterfamilias* was the domestic head of a household, one who possessed absolute and unquestionable authority. He had the authority to direct all of the members of the household (including his wife, children, and servants) in their social, legal, and religious affairs. He was expected to maintain the moral propriety and well-being of his dependents and raise them to be good Roman citizens. In this context, parental imagery was also applied metaphorically to a variety of authority figures in that society, including political leaders and philosophers. For instance, when an individual had a principal role in founding or saving the state, the citizens would attribute to him a paternal role as the "father" and provider for his people.

The cultural context contributed by both the Old Testament Scriptures and Greco-Roman society meant that the Corinthians would readily understand the significance of Paul applying a paternal image to himself. His choice of this imagery is also suggestive of the special relationship that he saw himself as enjoying with the Corinthians, one that is marked by privilege and protection.

It is such a relationship that he envisions continuing to share with them, for their good instruction, maturity, and protection.

Now, it is probably true that most Christian pastors today cannot be regarded as parents of their congregations in the same way that Paul referred to himself as a father of the Corinthians, one who had brought them to faith in Christ. However, there are aspects of this metaphor that remain most relevant and instructive. For just as being a biological parent is not limited to the task of conceiving a child and bringing her into the world, so being a pastor is not restricted to the task of founding a congregation through the initial efforts of evangelistic or missionary preaching. In fact, for both roles the greater task remains that of nurturing and caring for the "offspring" in the coming years. The promises and demands of the gospel need to be applied and worked out in the lives of the believers. Paul's fatherly example can assure a pastor that such faithful parenting will do much to enable the spiritual children to grow and to thrive.

A Fatherly Figure

When Paul regarded the Corinthians, he saw the indisputable evidence of his work. Years before, he was the first to preach the gospel among them. By visits and letters he then helped to build up the congregation in faith and to safeguard them from doctrinal and moral error. Paul describes the Corinthians as a testimony to his strenuous labors: "You are our epistle written in our hearts, known and read by all men" (2 Cor. 3:2).

As their spiritual father, Paul longs to stay involved with them in the coming years. In fact, it would be wrong for him to be an absentee father and to show a lack of concern for the Corinthians. He wants to give good direction to his household even when his children have matured and grown into adults. At that time, a son was expected to carry on the values of his father and to perpetuate the family name. With this cultural expectation in mind, Paul wants the Corinthians to imitate him, including his values and priorities. If necessary, he will be very direct in his teaching, speaking candidly with his children as is a father's prerogative. Paul is willing to give his children whatever direction is necessary, including the use of discipline or correction if he thought that this would lead to their progress in the faith (see 2 Cor. 10:6). Indeed, in this letter—in what might be said to be the true style of a parent!—Paul alternates warm compliments and affirmations with stern threats and admonitions.

His fatherly disposition is especially apparent in the passage we have already quoted, 2 Corinthians 6:11–13, where Paul writes to the congregation, "We have spoken openly to you, our heart is wide open. You are not restricted by us, but you are restricted by your own affections. Now in return for the same (I speak as to children), you also be open" (cf. 7:2). He wants his spiritual children to know that all his pastoral labors are intended to bring about a greater level of maturity. If they will be open and accepting of him in love—as he has been toward them—God will bless their relationship with stability and growth in Christ.

While Paul insists on his paternal authority in this letter, he refuses to exercise it in an imperious manner. In that cultural context, the relationship of father and child was inherently one of a superior and an inferior, but this did not necessarily mean that the structure was tyrannical. Indeed, the Pauline "family dynamic" is shaped in all things by love. This attitude was already intimated in Paul's words to this congregation in 1 Corinthians, when instead of taking the forceful tone of an authoritative *paterfamilias*, he speaks of desiring to adopt a gracious approach toward them: "What do you want? Shall I come to you with a rod, or in love and a spirit of gentleness?" (1 Cor. 4:21). He expresses a similar sentiment in 2 Corinthians 1:24, "*Not that we have dominion over your faith*, but are fellow workers for your joy." This loving paternal approach is much in evidence when we look at other features of Paul's attitude toward the Corinthians in this letter, namely, his gentleness in nurturing, his jealousy for their purity, his joy in their faith, his confidence in their responding, his prayer for their perfection, and his love for them as congregation.

Gentleness in Nurturing

In the complicated backstory of 2 Corinthians, Paul had been accused of being aggressive in what he wrote to them (2 Cor. 10:9–10). Although he undoubtedly has hard things to say to the Corinthians in this particular letter, he still manifests a spirit of gentleness. For instance, he writes, "I…am pleading with you by the meekness and gentleness of Christ" (v. 1). Paul fears that he may again have to be severe with them, but he hesitates; he wants the Corinthians to become aware of their fragile spiritual situation and to amend their conduct accordingly. To this end he will address them in a tender way. By this approach, he is deliberately contrasting himself with his verbally—even physically!—abusive counterparts in Corinth (11:20). He also wants to counter the accusation that he had been trying to frighten them and to correct the notion that his demeanor of gentleness was equivalent to cowardice (10:10). Ultimately, as Paul states in 2 Corinthians 10:1, he was basing himself on Christ as a model, for Jesus exemplified gentleness and forbearance in His earthly relationships. A pastor who imitates the model of Jesus will seek to convince rather than command.

Earlier in the letter Paul appeals to this gentle quality of his ministry: "But in all things we commend ourselves as ministers of God: in much patience…by longsuffering, by kindness, by the Holy Spirit, by sincere love" (2 Cor. 6:4–6). With self-assurance he insists that his character is basically devoid of any defects that would compromise his ministry. And consistent with this patient and kind attitude was Paul's concern to nurture the Corinthians toward spiritual maturity. He will take the time that is necessary to teach them, sensitive to those areas where they are still lacking. Although using a different image, Paul conveys the same sense when he compares himself to a caring mother, as we saw in 1 Thessalonians 2:7, "But we were gentle among you, just as a nursing mother cherishes her own children." A pastor who reflects on his role as a loving parent to his congregation will conclude that he should treat the members with this same kind of attitude.

This trait of gentleness can come to expression in many different moments of ministry. For example, a pastor can give instruction to his church through preaching in a spirit of honesty and gentleness. The difficulty is that it is easy to be a bully from the pulpit. A pastor can make things hard for the congregation by repeatedly stressing the serious duties of the Christian life and grimly pointing out the countless ways in which the congregation fails. While pastors must of course be guided by Scripture in their exhortations, they should also strive to be fair and gentle with Christ's people. Part of this approach is realizing that one extraordinarily good sermon will not clear up a contested doctrinal issue or set everyone permanently on the path of holiness. Caring for the family of God through preaching requires great patience and continual instruction. A gentle pastor will also not expect the congregation to do anything that he himself does not do. For instance, does the pastor literally pray "without ceasing" (1 Thess. 5:17), and does he never spend a minute of the day frivolously, and does he witness to every nonbeliever he meets? A pastor who realizes his own imperfections and struggles and yet strives to please God will be gentle with his "children" when bringing them the Word in preaching.

Similarly, gentleness in pastoral care means having a tender heart for Christ's people. Knowing his responsibility to care for a person well, a gentle pastor will listen carefully and patiently, trying to understand him or her before praying and offering guidance from Scripture. In a tender spirit, a pastor will consider the complexities of members' backgrounds, their present positions, their weaknesses and struggles, and then he will seek to show them God's grace. Paul says in Philippians 4:5, "Let your gentleness be known to all men"— an exhortation that pastors, too, surely need to heed. A gentle pastor will seek to comfort the hurting and reassure the troubled, to dry tears and to lighten loads.

Jealousy for the Congregation's Purity
A second aspect of Paul's fatherly concern for the Corinthians is his jealousy for their spiritual purity. He writes in 2 Corinthians 11:2:

"For I am jealous for you with godly jealousy. For I have betrothed you to one husband, that I may present you as a chaste virgin to Christ." This is an image that probably has its basis in the Old Testament metaphor of God as His people's bridegroom and Israel as His bride (e.g., Isa. 54:1–6; Ezek. 16; Hos. 1–3). In the New Testament, this image is filled out by the reality of the church as the bride, with Jesus as her heavenly bridegroom (Eph. 5:22–23; Rev. 19:7; 21:2, 9). In 2 Corinthians 11, Paul sees that he has a paternal role in safeguarding the purity of the church, Jesus's bride.

To understand this task, we can think of how in many cultures there is a moment of presentation when a woman gets married. For instance, in Western cultures the bride appears at the end of the aisle in church, her father at her side, then slowly walks to the front and to her bridegroom. Maybe a veil is lifted from her face, and the father presents her to her husband-to-be. Leading up to this significant moment, a bride will make many preparations, tending to her dress, hair, face, flowers, and jewelry. But in the case of the church, the bride can do nothing to make herself beautiful—it is Christ's work to make her lovely. The church is the unfaithful bride: contaminated by sin, repulsive in character, with nothing to offer. Yet this is our Husband's great love: He cleanses and sanctifies us so that He can present us "a glorious church, not having spot or wrinkle or any such thing" (Eph. 5:27). The church is like the most stunning bride through her union with Christ. Because of His sacrificial love, there will remain no defect of sin, no stain of worldliness, not even the smallest spot to spoil the church's purity.

As the servant of Christ and the father of the Corinthians, Paul says that he earnestly desires to preserve the purity of his "daughter." In that time, fathers typically had the responsibility of arranging the marriages of their daughters to worthy suitors. Paul fears that this purpose was in danger of being thwarted by the cunning tricks of his opponents, whom Paul likens to the serpent who deceived Eve in the garden of Eden (2 Cor. 11:3). Whether or not the Corinthians had in fact been seduced and had committed spiritual adultery, Paul takes on the weighty duty of protecting the honor and chastity of his daughter (cf. Deut. 22:13–21). He will attempt to ward off any attacks and deflect any inappropriate advances. This is a task that Paul as the bride's father takes very seriously, for he shares God's desire to see the full eschatological union between Christ and His church. As he waits for that day, Paul seeks to promote the love, faithfulness, and submission of Christ's church, particularly when these things are being sorely threatened.

The purity of the congregation's faith and the faithfulness of her commitment should be of paramount concern for a pastor today. There are any number of threats to the spiritual well-being of the church. These dangers take the form of erroneous teachings about such topics as human origins, the Bible's authority, or Christ's atoning work. In addition, there are the worldly temptations that constantly beset members of the church. Fatherly jealousy for the church's purity calls a pastor to directly confront the dangers of temptation and heresy. He will endeavor to protect the believers from threats to their faithfulness by teaching doctrinal discernment and by warning them against the devil's seductions. If a pastor truly values what Christ has accomplished for His bride in making her holy, then he will be deeply concerned for preserving the spiritual integrity of his congregation, that they might be pure for their God and Savior.

Joy in the Congregation's Faith

Paul's fatherly concern for the Corinthians means that he will also rejoice in their faith and obedience. His joy in the believers is expressed in several passages. Early in the letter, he implies that by continuing his work among them—as difficult as the work has been—he will eventually enjoy its fruit with great delight: "I determined this within myself, that I would not come again to you in sorrow.... And I wrote this very thing to you, lest, when I came, I should have sorrow over *those from whom I ought to have joy*" (2 Cor. 2:1–3). By their good response to the gospel of Christ, the Corinthians could turn his sorrow into joy. And as he considers the growing likelihood of this possibility, Paul is glad: "Therefore I rejoice that I have confidence in you in everything" (7:16). While their faithfulness would certainly increase his own joy, Paul wanted the Corinthians, too, to experience a renewed delight in the gospel: "[We] are fellow workers for *your* joy" (1:24). Through a restored relationship with God through Christ, the Corinthians would have every reason to rejoice in the Lord (cf. Phil. 4:4).

Once more, the root of this joy can be located in Paul's view of himself as the Corinthians' father in the faith. Like a proud father who says that his children are his joy because of their godly character and developing abilities, Paul will rejoice in his converts' faith. It is his expectation that those whom he is diligently serving in Corinth will afford him lasting spiritual pleasure through their faith and repentance. This is underlined by what Paul writes elsewhere, "I am exceedingly joyful in all our tribulation" (2 Cor. 7:4). This joy was particularly inspired by the positive report from Titus, who had recently come back to Paul from visiting the troubled congregation: "He told us of your earnest desire, your mourning, your zeal for me, *so that I rejoiced even more*" (7:7). In other letters, too, Paul speaks of the joy that he experiences when his congregations live by faith or repent from sin (e.g., Phil. 4:1; 1 Thess. 3:9). The Corinthians had caused him much regret, yet with more positive developments in the congregation recently he can say, "Now I rejoice, not that you were made sorry, but that your sorrow led to repentance" (2 Cor. 7:9).

These joy-filled statements illustrate the nature of Paul's pastoral relationship with his congregation. He identifies so closely with the Corinthians that their weaknesses and strengths, struggles and labors, become his own (see also 11:28–29), while their progress is a sure reason for his delight. The theological foundation of this perspective is the work of Christ, who identified Himself with the sinners He came to aid, seeking to restore them to spiritual wholeness before God (Phil. 2:7; Heb. 2:14). In the same spirit, Paul hopes that the anguish he previously suffered on account of the Corinthians will be displaced by this burgeoning joy as they repent from wrongdoing and grow into Christ.

In a similar way, there is much that can bring joy to pastors today. When he sees God's continued work in his congregation, a pastor can delight in the people's growth in faith and their devotion to Christian service. Particularly when someone has been living in sin, there can be great joy when that person repents and resolves anew to follow Christ. Indeed, seated in every pew on a given Sunday, there is cause for pastoral joy: earnest children, committed young people, godly husbands and wives, recovering addicts, steadfast seniors, and many more. A pastor sometimes has occasion to learn about the quiet acts of kindness done by his people, those who find ways to bless the needy, support the lonely, and encourage the troubled. In every ministry there will inevitably be moments of despair and times of joylessness, but it is fitting that a pastor remembers to rejoice, noticing the many ways that God is working in his congregation. Learning to see the miraculous effects of the Holy Spirit and the life-changing power of the Scriptures among God's children, a fatherly pastor can foster within himself a spirit of joy.

Confidence in the Congregation's Response

Despite the difficulties that have hounded his relationship with the Corinthians, Paul does not surrender to pessimism. On the contrary, he regularly speaks of his confidence that they will respond rightly to his teaching and pastoral care. In 2 Corinthians 7:4 he says, "Great is my boasting on your behalf." As a fatherly pastor regarding his beloved offspring, he voices the certainty that the Corinthians will continue to move in the right direction. He is sure that their faith in Christ will be expressed in renewed obedience to the Lord's commandments. Later, when speaking of the collection for the needy church in Jerusalem, Paul likewise speaks of his confidence that the Corinthians will be willing to give generously to support their fellow believers: "I know your willingness, about which I boast of you to the Macedonians...and your zeal has stirred up the majority" (9:2).

It is striking that Paul speaks here so boldly about the church of Corinth. He says that he is certain of their good response, even proud of their charitable spirit, though this has been a troubled, divided, legalistic, rebellious, immoral, and ungrateful congregation—a congregation that has shown a conspicuous lack of confidence in Paul as their pastor. But Paul's confidence is based not on the Corinthians' giftedness, nor on his ability to pastor them, but rather on Christ's sustaining power and God's faithfulness. He tells them that he is glad that "by faith you stand" (1:24), and if they keep trusting in God, he is sure that they will continue to stand firm. His enthusiasm for the evidence of God's grace among them reveals Paul's heart for these believers. He does not abandon the foundering pastor-congregation relationship, but he is consistently positive about seeing its eventual restoration and enjoying the fruit that will result.

Such a pastoral confidence is still fitting today. To be sure, there are sometimes reasons for pastoral pessimism. With the stubbornness of human pride and the lurking danger of complacency, with hearts that naturally gravitate toward idolatry and unbelief, will believers, one can wonder, really endure until the day of Jesus's return? Humanly speaking, you would not think so. If a pastor and his congregation are honest, it does not always look good—not for the pastor, and not for the congregation. But the broken church is still Christ's church, and the Spirit working in them is Christ's Spirit. By God's mighty intervention, despite all our weakness and sin, He has promised that we will continue to stand fast and even to grow. This promise can provide a pastor with quiet confidence as he regards his congregation: they are God's work, and God is faithful.

Prayers for the Congregation's Perfection

The caring attitude of "Father Paul" toward the Corinthians is also seen in the prayers that he offers on their behalf. Knowing that his ministerial labors are nothing without God's blessing, Paul brings the needs of the believers before his Father in heaven. In fact, his intercessory praying is a regular feature of the relationship that he enjoys with each of the churches he established (see, e.g., Eph. 3:14–19; Phil. 1:3–11; 1 Thess. 3:9–13). His prayers are not general in purpose or content, but specific in their cause, focused on Paul's concern for a continuation of the work he has carried out among these particular believers. He desires that the gospel will be advanced among those whom he had evangelized and ministered to, and he commits this desire to God in prayer.

What is true for Paul's relationship with other churches is also true for his bond with the Corinthians. His prayers in 2 Corinthians are not as lengthy as those in some of his other letters, but Paul does intimate to the Corinthians that he makes it a regular practice to pray for them. Having challenged the congregation to examine itself to see whether they are "in the faith" (2 Cor. 13:5), Paul writes, "I pray to God that you do no evil" (v. 7). Paul might have been praying for his renewed acceptance among the Corinthians as an apostle and pastor, but he also does not neglect to pray that they would be preserved in holiness. Two verses later, Paul again assures the Corinthians of his ongoing intercession to God on their behalf: "For we are glad when we are weak and you are strong. *And this also we pray*, that you may be made complete" (v. 9). Paul is glad for their good reaction to some of his admonitions, but he wants to see the continuation of this. Full restoration in Corinth would require a complete return to scriptural values, a rejection of the false apostles, and a sustained pursuit of holiness. As their pastor, Paul desires that they would have a strong and robust faith, and this is a longing that moves him to bring the needs of this church before God in prayer.

Simultaneous with his prayers for the Corinthians, Paul seeks their prayers for himself. An implied request for prayer is heard in 2 Corinthians 1:10–11: "We trust that He will still deliver us, *you also helping together in prayer for us*, that thanks may be given by many persons on our behalf for the gift granted to us through many." Aware of the numerous dangers that were threatening his pastoral work among them, Paul exhorts the Corinthians to pray for him. This request, too, is akin to his practice in letters to other congregations, in which he regularly asks for their support through intercessions for his ministry (see, e.g., Rom. 15:30; Eph. 6:19–20; Phil. 1:19). Through prayers from and for the congregation and their pastor, the work of Christ in His church will continue and will be blessed.

Following the example of Paul, a pastor should pray for the congregation in his care. It may be a prayer for restoration in line with

Paul's prayer for the Corinthians (2 Cor. 13:9), when a pastor asks God to grant a return to scriptural truth and fidelity to Christ after a period of unfaithfulness. Or a pastor may regularly pray for the congregation's growth in love, for their spiritual insight, for an attitude of humble service, and for their resistance in the face of temptation. As many and as varied as the church's needs, so should be a pastor's prayers.

While probably every Christian—and every pastor—will be quick to affirm the importance of prayer, there is a persistent inclination to neglect this spiritual discipline. In ministry, too, it is an activity that can easily be sidelined by the pressing obligations of the hour: an urgent pastoral visit to make, another sermon to craft, and an elders' meeting to prepare for. A pastor is expected to be a *doer*, and the long list of things waiting to be accomplished each week can leave little time for intentional and focused prayer. But with a humble dependence on God's blessing and with a father's heart for his children, a pastor will spend time regularly praying for those in his care.

Love for the Congregation

Throughout 2 Corinthians Paul's attitude toward the congregation is characterized by a generous and heartfelt love, one that resembles the sparkling expressions of pastoral affection in Paul's other letters. For instance, he writes to the Philippians, "Therefore, my beloved and longed-for brethren, my joy and crown, so stand fast in the Lord, beloved" (4:1). Or consider Paul's poignant words to the Thessalonian congregation as he reflects on the love that moved and shaped his ministry among them: "So, affectionately longing for you, we were well pleased to impart to you not only the gospel of God, but also our own lives, because you had become dear to us" (1 Thess. 2:8). Clearly, Paul was a pastor who loved his people!

While Paul is definitely not reticent to express his affection for the churches, it is especially striking in the case of the Corinthians. Despite the troubles that have vexed their pastor-congregation relationship, and regardless of the Corinthians' recent mistreatment of him, he actually avows his pastoral affection more frequently in this letter than in any other. For instance, this love is apparent in

2 Corinthians 2:4, where Paul reflects on the painful letter that he had previously sent: "For out of much affliction and anguish of heart I wrote to you, with many tears, not that you should be grieved, *but that you might know the love which I have so abundantly for you.*" He abhors the idea that his past actions were motivated by a desire to inflict injury or offense. Rather, it was the opposite: his pleading admonitions were an expression of his deep concern for the Corinthians. Again, in 2 Corinthians 11:11, he asks them rhetorically why he was willing to undergo the hardship of self-support: "Why? Because I do not love you? God knows!" This protest reflects Paul's view of the Corinthians and at the same time expresses his reaction to the suggestion that he did not love this congregation. Paul wants to convince the Corinthians that he always seeks their interests and that he has treated them with an unselfish love. He draws attention to this quality of his ministry in 2 Corinthians 6 as well, as part of his claim for commendation: "In all things we commend ourselves as ministers of God...*by sincere love*" (vv. 4–6). The phrase rendered "sincere love" literally translates as "unhypocritical love." Paul has always tried to minister to the Corinthians without pretense or deception.

It is, of course, easy to say, "I love you," but much harder to show it. So more than just verbally declaring his love, Paul reminds the Corinthians of his many tangible contributions to a loving relationship. For instance, he brought them the gospel (10:14), he honored them at his own expense (11:7), he has been committed to building them up (12:19), he sacrificed himself for their benefit (v. 15), he has not taken advantage of them (v. 17), he has been a selfless parent (v. 14), he has not failed to admonish them (v. 20), and he has challenged them to lead a faithful life (13:5). In view of all his work for their benefit, Paul makes the paradoxical observation in 12:15, "And I will very gladly spend and be spent for your souls; though the more abundantly I love you, the less I am loved." To Paul, it seems that the closer he has moved toward the Corinthians, the more they have pulled back. He knows that at least some of the Corinthians were loyal to him (7:7), yet Paul pleads with the congregation for a renewed display of their sincere love: "You are not restricted by us, but you are restricted by your own affections." Then he adds, "Open your hearts to us" (6:12; 7:2). Even in asking for their reciprocal affection, Paul exposes his vulnerability. He is willing to be seen as weak and needy in the hopes that his appeal may result in their spiritual growth.

It is an abiding truth that love involves a person in the lives of others in a selfless way. In particular, a pastor's fatherly love is expressed in a wholehearted investment in his church's spiritual welfare. Many years ago in seminary, I remember one of my professors sharing the adage: "People don't care how much you know; they want to know how much you care." It is not as though theological knowledge and loving affection are mutually exclusive, but a practical concern for the congregation is indispensable for faithful ministry. A pastor undoubtedly possesses much knowledge, in most cases having received years of secondary and postsecondary education and having read vast amounts of Christian theology. Still, there should be no question in the minds of the congregants whether their pastor genuinely cherishes them. Even when admonitions or warnings must be given, a pastor's dealings with the church should be characterized by love. In every circumstance, a true pastor seeks the good of the believers entrusted to his care.

It is true that the more we love people, the more we will share in their pains and griefs. This was Paul's experience, that he suffered because of a sympathetic sharing in the weaknesses and struggles of his spiritual children (see 11:28–29). A similar suffering is likely to be experienced by any dedicated pastor when a congregation's losses, setbacks, and troubles are felt by him at a personal level. In Christ, these people become dear to a pastor and he wants to move toward them in love. At the same time, a caring pastor will probably experience that some people can seem almost unlovable; there will be some members who annoy and frustrate, who resist any efforts to help, and who answer pastoral kindness with resentment. But Paul's example among the Corinthians teaches pastors to persist in love. We love Christ, so we will gladly do his work. We love Christ, so we will keep loving his people.

Conclusion: Open Hearts

Marveling at Paul's persistent and selfless love for the Corinthians is an apt place to conclude this chapter on fatherly pastoring. By God's design, the bonds of a pastor and his congregation run deep. Friendly, even familial, affection requires sacrifice and is often attended by pain. But much more than this, such love can bring great joy. It is a delight when a pastor is devoted to his church with a jealous, prayerful, gentle, and loving spirit—and when the church receives his nurture and care with gratitude and openness. Such an openhearted relationship (cf. 6:13) will bring mutual blessing to the pastor and his congregation and will result in glory to God.

CHAPTER 4

PREACHING FOR THE GLORY OF CHRIST

For we are to God the fragrance of Christ among those who are being saved and among those who are perishing.
—2 CORINTHIANS 2:15

Perhaps you listen to preaching every Sunday and have done so for many years. Perhaps you preach every Sunday and have done so for many years. In a church that has long valued preaching, there is probably a quiet assumption that everyone knows what it means to preach. But what *does* it mean? In our society today, the word often has a negative tone: "Don't go preaching at me," someone snaps at a moralistic friend or judgmental neighbor. There is a natural resistance to the notion of being told by someone else what to believe or how to behave. And it is difficult to leave that resistance at the church door on Sunday mornings. Who gives the balding, middle-aged man at the front of the auditorium the right to speak with authority into my life? So it is good to contemplate what God's Word says about this essential activity.

When we (very) briefly consider how the New Testament speaks about preaching, we learn a few key truths. A fundamental passage for the pastor's preaching task is the apostolic command in 2 Timothy 4:2, "Preach the word!" In this text the original Greek verb describes bringing a message on behalf of someone else. For example, in Paul's day runners would go ahead of a traveling king or governor into the cities and villages in order to announce his coming and make known his will—they would literally "preach." In the New Testament, "preaching" means proclaiming on behalf of someone in a position of supremacy and authority. Still today, a preacher in a very real sense is an ambassador who speaks for the coming King (cf. 2 Cor. 5:19–20). A preacher brings a message from his heavenly Sender and he gets people ready to receive their Lord.

If the apostle Paul had an official job description, this would have been the task that was bolded, underlined, and put in the uppermost place: *preaching.* What was Paul called to do? And what is every pastor called to do? Consider what Paul said to the Corinthians in his first letter about his labors in their midst: "For I determined not to know anything among you except Jesus Christ and Him crucified" (1 Cor. 2:2). This was his preaching ministry's singular focus: proclaiming Christ, the anointed King. And a preacher today remains under divine compulsion to preach the message of salvation through the crucified and resurrected Jesus, for Christ is the hope in our trouble, the relief in our misery, and He is our righteousness and our salvation! This is the awesome ministry that was entrusted to Paul and to every preacher. In this chapter, we will explore Paul's task, as a new covenant minister, of preaching Christ, how he continued to preach despite facing severe criticism, and how pastors today may bring the same glorious gospel.

Preaching the New Covenant in Christ

Paul speaks of the all-surpassing glory of his preaching ministry in 2 Corinthians 3–6. Here he first sets up a contrast between the nature of the old and new covenants and the accessibility of their respective messages. Without question, the old covenant was magnificent—witness the terrifying glory of Mount Sinai and hear the thunder and lightning (2 Cor. 3:7–11; cf. Ex. 19:16). And see how the face of Moses shone with a brilliant but unbearable radiance after his meeting with the Lord God of Israel (2 Cor. 3:7, 13; cf. Ex. 34:29–30). That was Sinai: God's revelation in spectacle and splendor. When the holy and living God comes near, the creation itself has to react, and every human bystander must be moved with fear and trembling. Such is the majesty of God. It cannot be toned down or diminished; His perfect holiness is overwhelming. To be sure, this holy LORD is not some ogre who is eager to crush His people for the slightest misstep, for He wants to fellowship with His people by entering into a covenant with them. Even so, the LORD is immutable in His character as the holy, just, and almighty God. He is who He is, clothed in glory and splendor (Ex. 3:14). As a result, there was great fear at Mount Sinai; it was forty days of shock and awe (Heb. 12:18–21).

What happened at Sinai laid bare just how far from the living God is sinful mankind. No one may approach Him, though not because He doesn't want to be approached. Rather, the right way needs to be opened—only when human sin has been properly dealt with and sinners have been effectively cleansed. And ultimately, the old covenant was not able to provide that possibility. Keeping the law imperfectly would not meet the flawless standard of God's holiness, and neither would making endless animal offerings ever be sufficient to atone for Israel's sins and transgressions (Heb. 10:4). In every respect, the old covenant was provisional and anticipatory, and its "glory was passing away" (2 Cor. 3:7). Thus already in the days of the Old Testament, God promised a new covenant (Jer. 31:31–34; Ezek. 36:26–27), a covenant which was finally inaugurated with the perfect sacrifice of Jesus.

Paul impresses onto the Corinthians that the new covenant through Christ is entirely superior: "For it is the God who commanded light to shine out of darkness, who has shone in our hearts to give the light of the knowledge of the glory of God in the face of Jesus Christ" (2 Cor. 4:6). Instead of seeing the Judge's face darkened with wrath, sinners are allowed to see the Father's face beaming with kindness in Christ. Instead of being turned away from God's presence and into the terror that exists apart from Him, sinners are welcomed into the peace of the Father's household. While the Israelites were held back, standing behind the barriers at Mount Sinai and behind the barriers of the temple, in Christ we are now allowed to approach God's presence with a sure boldness. Those who are graciously included in the new covenant can stand in the radiance of God's majesty, "beholding…the glory of the Lord" (3:18). How far from God is sinful mankind, yet how very near to God have believers been brought through Jesus Christ! Through the sacrifice of His Son, God has bridged the divide and torn down the once-impassable barrier of our sin. He has announced that sinners can be forgiven and He has welcomed believers into loving fellowship. Through Christ Jesus, His new covenant church may worship Him with a new closeness, serve Him with a new strength, and call on Him with a new confidence (cf. Heb. 10:19–21).

The glory of God the Father has been revealed in a stunning new way by Christ, and now His word of salvation ought to be preached by His appointed messengers. As Paul writes about the privilege of this work, "God…made us sufficient as ministers of the new covenant" (2 Cor. 3:5–6). In themselves, Christ's preachers are lowly, but they are allowed to speak with great boldness. Indeed, if you have something to say, there is nothing better than being confident in your message. One could compare it to salespeople, for the best salesperson is the one who can speak with great conviction about the product he is selling: "This minivan has the best safety rating in the industry!" "This building product really is top-tier!" Having a message that is infinitely more significant than people-movers and plywood, the preacher of the new covenant in Christ can be forthright in his preaching: "Since we have such hope, we use great boldness of speech" (v. 12). Every Sunday a preacher can announce to his congregation: "This is the gospel of your redemption; this is the Word of truth about the glory of God!" The message is life-saving and life-renewing as the preacher tells about the redemption that is freely available by faith in Christ. Because it is so indispensable, the gospel is not something that the preacher is allowed to keep to himself or to preach without enthusiasm or passion. No, he is under divine compulsion to share the message in an urgent and persuasive manner; as Paul writes in 1 Corinthians, "Necessity is laid upon me; yes, woe is me if I do not preach the gospel!" (9:16).

Preaching Christ Crucified

This was a longing that Paul had expressed more than once to the Corinthians, that he yearned to preach Christ. What else could he say, and whom else could he proclaim? Likewise, a pastor today must be determined to maintain this as first and foremost on his list of duties. It is the high calling and incredible privilege of Christian ministry to preach about the one Person who can make a true difference in the life of the sinner. Preaching will probably always be under the pressures of societal conformity—expected to be entertaining, to provide quick fixes to the problems of daily existence, or to be endlessly affirming. But when a preacher is focused on announcing the finished atoning work of Jesus, he is no longer compelled to be innovative in content, politically correct, or entertaining: "I preach Christ and Him crucified."

It is a deceptively simple way to put it, of course: Preach Christ! It does not mean that preachers will speak only of Christ, that every sermon will have Christ in the theme and Christ in all three (or four) points. But a faithful preacher will always establish and center his message on Christ, because in some sense all of Scripture speaks about Him (John 5:39). In Christ, all the lines of history converge (Gal. 4:4). In Christ, everything in the universe holds together (Col. 1:17). Thus every time that the preacher comes to the pulpit and opens the Word, every eye ought to be fixed on Christ and Him alone (Heb. 12:2). Whatever the particular circumstances of God's people, whatever their felt needs at that moment, a preacher is called to bring the Word of Christ. Whatever the believer's worries, joys, temptations, and longings—the word of salvation can be spoken into his or her life with powerful effect. In Christ there is relief for people crushed by their guilt, joy for those troubled by anxiety, courage for those trapped in their addictions, help for the ones burdened in wrecked relationships, peace for believers facing death, and comfort for those who are grieving. There is hope, because for Christ's sake God has promised to help, forgive, and restore with the Father's lavish love.

Through the blessing of God the Holy Spirit, the activity of preaching Christ has an immense power. Probably any preacher with a few years of experience will be able to attest to seeing the transformative nature of the preached Word. The sermon might not have been perfect, and the person in the pew may have missed many of its fine exegetical points, yet he or she was still greatly encouraged or soundly exhorted. In fact, a preacher never really knows what lesson or exhortation his hearers will draw from the sermon, as a preacher often has little idea of what condition people are in as they listen, whether discouraged, lonely, content, joyful, fatigued, or resolute. Sometimes hearers will glean little more than one comment made in passing by the preacher, a simple allusion, an example or illustration, and God uses this snippet to speak His truth directly into their lives for a blessing. Knowing the power and capability of the preached Word when it is centered on Christ and faithful to the Scriptures, preachers should cherish the opportunity and necessity of imparting God's truth to God's people.

Speaking of Criticism

No account of preaching in 2 Corinthians would be complete without a consideration of how Paul had been sharply criticized for this central activity of his ministry. In the next chapter we will look at other criticisms of Paul, but here we note the Corinthians' disapproval of his preaching. His opponents lambasted him for a poor speaking ability: "He writes a strong letter," they said, "but in person he's a weakling. Think about his sermons—they don't amount to much at all" (cf. 2 Cor. 10:9–10). The rival ministers in Corinth compared the apostle to themselves because they evidently were polished speakers with impressive personalities, while Paul was awkward in character and stilted in speaking. He had apparently given some poor performances in situations of public speaking. Perhaps some in the congregation still remembered his preaching from the eighteen months that he first spent ministering in Corinth (Acts 18:11), or they recalled the sermons that he delivered during a subsequent visit to the church. Plainly, some aspects of his preaching were underscored by his opponents as being significantly inferior and wholly uninspiring.

Already in 1 Corinthians, Paul had responded to the slights and disparagements of his preaching ministry while in their midst: "When I came to you, [I] did not come with excellence of speech or of wisdom declaring to you the testimony of God. For I determined not to know anything among you except Jesus Christ and Him crucified. I was with you in weakness, in fear, and in much trembling. And my speech and my preaching were not with persuasive words of human wisdom, but in demonstration of the Spirit and of power, that your faith should not be in the wisdom of men but in the power of God" (1 Cor. 2:1–5). At least two years had elapsed since Paul wrote these words, but some of the criticism in 2 Corinthians is foreshadowed here, for he is being perceived as a feeble and timid person in his speaking, a man of "weakness," "fear," and "trembling." Now in the second letter, Paul indicates that these faults have been seized on with a vengeance in order to thrash his credibility. This is how he represents his critics' disparaging complaints: "'For his letters,' they say, 'are weighty and powerful, but his bodily presence is weak, and his speech contemptible'" (2 Cor. 10:10). By some he was evidently considered to be a deficient preacher. Perhaps it was because of shortfalls in his rhetorical training. Or perhaps it was because of his reluctance to use gimmicks and emotional tricks, as he says, "We have renounced the hidden things of shame, not walking in craftiness nor handling the word of God deceitfully" (4:2). Such factors were counted against the apostle and he had to endure the Corinthians' denigration, even as he again admits his lack of natural or acquired eloquence toward the end of the letter: "I am untrained in speech" (11:6).

Probably many pastors today would modestly acknowledge that they are not refined orators or naturally captivating speakers, but for Paul to freely acknowledge this shortcoming—even to boast about it!—is remarkable. At his time there was a high premium placed on rhetorical ability. The practice and expectations of rhetorical eloquence were pervasive in the first century, not only in the areas of politics, but also in philosophy and religion. As such, rhetoric was the final stage of education for a privileged Roman youth. Skill in oratory was a powerful status symbol, for positions of societal leadership were generally claimed by those who had the ability to persuade others. The Corinthians were judging their spiritual leaders by this key marker of status, a criterion which was fundamental to their vaunted "wisdom" (see 1 Cor. 1:20–22). This was a congregation who favored eloquence and neatly packaged oratory, what Paul calls the "wisdom of words" (1:17). To their view, the manner of presentation was far more important than the actual content. And if a speaker could not meet their self-styled standards for eloquence, then he was considered gravely inferior and probably not worth listening to.

This was a deficiency in Paul that some of the Corinthians would not overlook. Yet he did not hesitate to admit, "My speech and my preaching were not with persuasive words of human wisdom" (2:4). He decided to flout the cultural expectations for his preaching so that the gospel of Christ would not be jeopardized. For Paul saw that something far more crucial than external form or verbal style was at stake, namely, the gospel itself.

Preaching Themselves

The leaders who had infiltrated the congregation were good-looking and charismatic people, capable of delivering powerful sermons, and perhaps even adept at healings and speaking in tongues. Paul would have no objection to such things. As he insists to the Philippians with respect to the "rival" preachers at work in that congregation, "What then? Only that in every way, whether in pretense or in truth, Christ is preached; and in this I rejoice, yes, and will rejoice" (Phil. 1:18). But what about his Corinthian rivals? What were they preaching, and was Paul able to delight in their message?

Paul is almost certainly contrasting himself with his Corinthian opponents when he says, "For we do not preach ourselves, but Christ Jesus the Lord" (2 Cor. 4:5). The inference is that these other ministers were happily proclaiming *themselves*, seeking personal acclaim and adoration through their preaching. They probably wanted people lining up after the worship service to offer a fresh round of compliments. They liked to see the admiring glances and hear the whispered comments as they walked past, "There goes Pastor Demetrius. He's a noble man, a strong leader, and a polished speaker!" In their pulpit ministry, it was they who earned all the attention and praise.

And what was all this admiration without some financial gain? These ministers wanted the good income that accompanied the work of "religious professionals" in the congregation (cf. 2:17). But this meant that the ministers would be tempted to preach what the people wanted to hear. After all, you cannot expect financial patronage and material support if you cause offense and ruffle congregational feathers. On the other hand, if you tickle their ears with good stories and easy platitudes (cf. 2 Tim. 4:3–4), if you make it all neatly packaged and smoothly delivered, your efforts may well be rewarded with good monetary returns.

But Paul says that if these pastors are serving themselves, then they are not serving Christ. If these pastors are preaching themselves, then they are not preaching the cross. This is the fundamental reason that the Corinthians' criticism moved Paul to vigorously defend his ministry of preaching. He was eager to do so, not because the Corinthians were rejecting him, but because they were rejecting the gospel he preached. By repeatedly denigrating the messenger, they were ridiculing his message at the same time. For if you want a glitzy and glamorous preacher, you will probably want him to bring a clever and entertaining message—and this is simply not what the true gospel or true ministry is. Ministry is not about "preaching ourselves," for the message of Christ is so much more important and powerful than the weak human messenger who proclaims it.

False Expectations and True Power

The Corinthians had a hard time remembering the true measure of preaching, and the difficulty is ours as well: it is the problem of expectations. When it comes to preachers and pastors, we can embrace false ideals and improper standards. Just as in the days of the Corinthians, today much value is placed on a speaker's charisma, eloquence, and appearance. We probably all have a deep-seated preference for the superficial. We like best the things that look lovely and that sound pleasing, while we gravitate toward people who are outwardly appealing and agreeable.

This preference is probably a reflection of how Western culture has become a celebrity culture. Constant attention is given to the sacred stars of sports or music or movies, and we are continually fed "news" about the charismatic, exciting, accomplished, and good-looking people of the world. It is easy to dismiss all of this as inane worldliness, yet the values and moods of a celebrity culture can also sway the church. How are lowly and ordinary-looking preachers received in such a culture of fame and style? Slickness of performance can easily become primary, as polish is allowed to replace substance. Even within the context of many reliable websites for Christian resources and ministries, a local pastor has become just one humble voice among countless other authorities on Scripture. What is more, he has been brought into competition with YouTube preachers who are clearly excellent at what they do. How does a congregation view their modestly gifted pastor in comparison with all the skilled preachers and podcasters of our time?

If we have false expectations and improper standards for Christian ministry, then pastors and congregations alike should prepare to be disappointed. For the bottom line, Paul says, is that a preacher cannot preach himself. Ministry simply cannot be about him, but about the glory of God revealed in Christ. When a preacher is preaching, he may not build his message on the back of his own experiences and opinions. Neither should he constantly have one eye on the positive feedback he wants to receive—or even on the paycheck he wants to receive. For it is not about him, and it must never be! In Paul's view, such self-abnegation and admiration redirection actually make perfect sense. As he might say, "Of course we do not preach ourselves—we are but earthen vessels!" (cf. 2 Cor. 4:7). A pastor is a weak and breakable servant, a humble receptacle for the splendid treasure of Christ's gospel. Pastors have nothing to boast about, for they are frail and dependent creatures. Why would a pastor ever put himself at the center of attention when he has begun to realize that he is helpless and incompetent? He does not preach because he is a good preacher, but because he has been sent by Christ with a wondrous gospel to announce. A minister who has a grasp of true ministry realizes that it is not about him, but it is all about Jesus Christ. And because his identity is not found in his preaching but in the One who sends him, a minister will preach Christ boldly and unfailingly.

Consequently, a Christian preacher also does well to heed Paul's cautions against an impressive but empty oratory. This does not mean that preachers must eschew stylistic or rhetorical beauty while crafting and delivering their sermons. As Paul himself demonstrated in 2 Corinthians and his other letters, as well as in his sermons recorded in Acts, he clearly knew how to turn a phrase well and to construct a convincing argument. Yet this rhetorical skill was always subservient to the message Paul brought. As he affirmed in 1 Corinthians, "For Christ did not send me to baptize, but to preach the gospel, not with wisdom of words, lest the cross of Christ should be made of no effect" (1:17). He did not want eloquence to distract in any way from a focus on Christ's gospel; likewise, preachers today must remember that it is not the style or cleverness of their messages that will change people's lives, but only the truth and power of the gospel of Christ.

Paul's rivals may well have been better preachers than he was, but he loved the Corinthians more. And it is almost certainly true that a congregation listens better to a preacher when he is a pastor who knows them intimately and who cares for them sincerely. Such a meaningful and impactful pastor-congregation relationship can never be replaced by "following" an appealing preacher from another city or a teacher who has an impressive online platform.

Preaching the Fragrance of Christ

In his first letter to the Corinthians, Paul recalled the glorious gospel message of Christ's redeeming work that he brought to them during his initial visit to the city: "For I delivered to you first of all that which I also received: that Christ died for our sins according to the Scriptures, and that He was buried, and that He rose again the third day according to the Scriptures" (15:3–4). Paul's public speaking ability might have been lacking in some respects, but this did not prevent the true message of the crucified and risen Christ from being heard on his lips.

Reflecting on his preaching task in 2 Corinthians, Paul says that God is pleased to spread the "fragrance of life" through his proclamation of Christ. He asserts that the gospel is like a captivating scent that enlivens all who breathe it in: "For we are to God the fragrance of Christ among those who are being saved and among those who are perishing" (2 Cor. 2:15). When a preacher preaches like God wants him to preach, there is a certain smell that wafts through the auditorium: "the aroma of life leading to life" (v. 16). The gospel is something to breathe in, a smell you can savor. "The Fragrance of Christ" cannot be captured, bottled, and sold in the perfume section at a department store. But it is a beautiful scent, like when you come home from work and smell something delicious cooking on the stove or baking in the oven: fried onions or chocolate chip cookies—an aroma that brings a smile to your face. The gospel is the sweet fragrance of Christ, because its core message is the good news that God has reconciled sinners to Himself through His Son. It is the message that there is grace for the contrite, hope for the hopeless, and strength for the weak. It is the aroma of life, for the preaching of the gospel does nothing less than open the eternal kingdom of Jesus Christ.

And a preacher should remember that gospel preaching *always* gives off a scent. Even for those who reject it, the gospel has an odor, but then not the fragrance of life and beauty. For those who reject it, the gospel is "the aroma of death" (v. 16). For them, the gospel has the smell of a dead and decomposing body. You might say that it has the warning smell of propane: it is a most disagreeable stench, and that is not even the worst of it. If you fail to react, there is potential for personal injury, even disaster. Whenever it is not received in faith, the preaching of Christ gives off the smell of condemnation. It reeks of a person's failure to be reconciled to God their creator. If a person keeps hearing the gospel but does not believe it—and keeps loving sin more than loving Christ—the gospel of Christ warns and convicts, and it smells like death.

Preaching Jesus as Lord

As congregants listen to the preaching and receive its sweet comforts and encouragements and promises, they also have a duty and calling. No listener can be unresponsive to the Word they have heard because it is about Jesus, the Savior who redeems and the King who commands. This is how Paul sums up his message: "We preach Christ Jesus the Lord" (cf. 4:5). A "lord" has dominion over other people; he even owns them as his possession through the payment of a purchase price. Sinners gratefully acknowledge that Jesus poured out His precious blood for them, and that by paying this price He brought deliverance from condemnation (1 Peter 1:18–19). That Christ paid this price means He is our Lord, as Paul previously reminded the Corinthians: "Or do you not know that your body is the temple of the Holy Spirit who is in you, whom you have from God, and you are not your own? For you were bought at a price; therefore glorify God in your body" (1 Cor. 6:19–20). Through his preaching to the congregation and by his teaching through letters, Paul promoted the lordship of Christ among the Corinthians. In 1 Corinthians, for instance, Paul insisted on Christ's lordship over such things as sexuality and marriage, corporate worship and daily diet. In 2 Corinthians, Paul demonstrates how Jesus is Lord over our money, our relationships with unbelievers, and the life of our congregations.

Christ looks at a redeemed sinner's life and He says, "This is mine. Your life belongs to Me because I bought you completely with My precious blood." Thus the activity of preaching Christ must also make clear that the Lord Jesus now rules our home life, our personal finances, our leisure activities, and our employment—Christ has something to say about *all* of it. This is the consequence Paul draws out of Christ's redeeming death: "He died for all, that those who live should live no longer for themselves, but for Him who died for them and rose again" (2 Cor. 5:15). Every Sunday, those purchased by Christ's blood must hear that they now get to live for Him.

Preaching with Patience

Though they are entrusted with the high privilege of spreading the aroma of Christ and preaching Jesus as Lord, preachers are all faced with their own shortcomings, Sunday after Sunday. Probably every pastor is familiar with an unpleasant condition sometimes called the "Monday morning blues." When he goes back to his study on Monday, a pastor can feel mildly depressed. He is mulling over how he could have said so many things better, or how he forgot this or that point—in short, he is thinking that perhaps he is just not up to the job. As Paul himself agonizes, "Who is sufficient for these things?" (2:16). During the week, the pastor might have spent ten or twenty hours in sermon preparation, but all that time and effort evaporate in one tension-filled hour on Sunday. Was it worth it? Did he accomplish anything at all?

Even when a preacher is resolutely and faithfully preaching from week to week, at times it can seem like God's people are not listening. They might all sit quietly on Sunday morning and appear to be paying attention, but they don't ever seem to change. Everything stays just as it was before. So a preacher can become frustrated when he does not see the progress that he envisioned when he first started in this congregation. After three years, he knows that there are still judgmental attitudes among the members, and there is still a reluctance to share the gospel with their neighbors, or there is a neglect of the personal study of Scripture. Last Sunday he preached (what he considered) an almost flawless sermon, but still he wonders if it made any difference. Did anyone even hear what he said?

It is true that the "outcomes" of gospel preaching are hard to define and even more difficult to see. After years of preaching ministry, has there been a demonstrable life change among the hearers? Can you really measure an increase in holy learning? How do you quantify a congregation's growth in faith? Elsewhere Paul reminds us that the activity of preaching the Word calls for long-suffering and patience (2 Tim. 4:2). A preacher should keep bringing the Word, week after week, year after year, knowing that this is exactly what

Christ's people need. When the Word is faithfully preached, the Holy Spirit will take care of changing and growing the believers.

Besides everything else that will receive a pastor's attention in a given week or year of ministry, it remains true that the pulpit is the most important place for his work. Through preaching, God allows a pastor the opportunity to simultaneously and with divine authority address the entire congregation—including any visitors and seekers—and to address them all about matters that are eternally significant. Preaching is a unique opportunity to unfold the riches and beauty of God's Word, and to do so in a clear, accessible, and personal way. With Scripture open, and pointing the congregation to God's truth without apology, a pastor must make each sermon a faithful and Christ-centered exposition of God's Word. Thinking of the widely varied congregation in front of him—old and young, female and male, well-informed and simple, strong and weak—the pastor seeks to teach, correct, rebuke, and exhort each one. A sermon might only be half an hour or forty-five minutes in length, but this is the pastor's auspicious opportunity to impart sound instruction and encouragement for the six days that lie ahead, and hopefully for some time to come. He is weak, but his message is strong. And so he is compelled to preach his heart out every Sunday, exulting in Christ crucified and celebrating God's unchanging truth, then standing back and praying fervently as the congregation departs into another week.

—∞—

CHAPTER 5

FACING A BARRAGE
OF CRITICISM

For not he who commends himself is approved, but whom the Lord commends.
—2 CORINTHIANS 10:18

One of ministry's pernicious pains is the criticism that is leveled at a pastor. The critical comments might be applicable and fair, or they might be unjust and off base, but they will definitely come. A new pastor quickly learns that he can be the object of all kinds of criticism:

"You should go deeper into the text."

"Why isn't our congregation growing?"

"Less lecturing, more applying."

"Too bad you're not as dynamic as Pastor Dan."

"Can't you update the music? It's so 1750s."

Perhaps most painfully, a pastor's "Monday morning blues" can be exacerbated by a Monday morning email that rips to shreds the previous day's sermon. Writing behind the safety of a computer keyboard, a congregant boldly offers his view on how the pastor's flawed exegesis and artificial application meant that the sermon was a miserable failure that surely did not edify anyone in the congregation. And quite apart from the criticism that a pastor will receive for his preaching, he is also likely to attract disapproval for decisions made by the body of elders. A pastor is something of a lightning rod for criticism—the highest or most obvious point available to be struck in a storm—even when the reason for the complaint may not be his fault or decision alone. Being in the public eye opens up a pastor to extra scrutiny or criticism. Because criticism—both fair and unfair—is inevitable, a pastor must learn to respond to it wisely and patiently so that it does not unduly discourage but becomes an occasion for growth. And once again, Pastor Paul has valuable lessons to teach.

Corinthian Criticism

In an earlier chapter we saw how competing church leaders arose in Corinth and adversely influenced the congregation's view of the apostle. These opponents had challenged Paul's authority while elevating their own status, and many were swayed to doubt both Paul's personal ability as a pastor and his devotion to their spiritual welfare. Because Paul considers that the gospel itself is at stake in this controversy, he feels compelled to respond to the criticisms. Even so, reacting puts him in a difficult place. If he says too little, he won't be able to address the issues properly and the congregation will drift further away. If he says too much, they will probably accuse him of being heavy-handed (again). Pastors may be able to relate to the awkward position in which Paul finds himself: needing to respond to criticism without boasting in himself, being excessively defensive, or damaging an already tenuous relationship.

The root of the attacks on Paul was his opponents' determination to compare him to themselves. They judged that Paul simply did not measure up to their self-fabricated standard for ministry. This is seen when Paul writes in his own defense with a clearly ironic tone: "For we dare not class ourselves or compare ourselves with those who commend themselves" (2 Cor. 10:12). Paul's opponents had even produced letters of recommendation written by persons unknown to us; these were approving letters that served as their so-called credentials among the Corinthians (3:1). This strategy was consistent with the competitive spirit of Corinth's secular society, in which boasting of personal strength and exploiting relationships were means by which to attain preeminence over others.

While it is hard to be sure exactly what standard had been set by Paul's rivals, for the Corinthians the central question seems to have been whether he could claim the same experiences and skills as these other ministers. The first aspect of these comparisons was how they boasted of their miraculous powers and ecstatic visions. These spiritual experiences greatly distinguished the new leaders from the reputedly non-mystical Paul—a charge to which he responds in 2 Corinthians 12:1, "I will come to visions and revelations of the Lord."

A second aspect of their critical comparisons is related to his speaking. As we saw in the previous chapter, Paul had admitted in 1 Corinthians that he had a weakness in regard to preaching: "My speech and my preaching were not with persuasive words of human wisdom" (1 Cor. 2:4). In that culture, a wise person was expected to be eloquent and educated, to have an impressive demeanor and attractive appearance. This was a requirement that the Corinthians judged Paul as having failed to meet. While he came across as gallant in his written words, he appeared cowardly when present with them and expressing himself orally (2 Cor. 10:1). In this letter he echoes their demeaning charge: "'His letters,' they say, 'are weighty and powerful, but his bodily presence is weak, and his speech contemptible'" (v. 10). The Corinthians were troubled by this apparent inconsistency in the apostle's character, and it caused them to question his legitimacy as a leader.

Third, the reference to Paul being unimpressive in person (v. 10) has sometimes been understood to mean that his opponents were attacking features of his physical appearance. However, it is less likely that they were casting aspersions on his personal or physical condition, and more likely that the target of their ridicule was his general deportment—which was a much more serious charge. Paul certainly did not present himself to the Corinthians as a strong or imposing figure; already in his first letter he had conceded that his character might not have made a strong impression: "I was with you in weakness, in fear, and in much trembling" (1 Cor. 2:3). Now in his second letter, he speaks at length about his personal sufferings and about his condition of debility or weakness. As with his low social position and his inferior rhetorical ability, this personal weakness was a serious strike against him. Without strength, a man's honor would suffer. This reality makes Paul's extensive boasting in 2 Corinthians about his various hardships all the more puzzling to us. Unless, of course, Paul could adequately explain to the Corinthians the true nature of his suffering, which is what he sets out to do.

Fourth, the Corinthians judged that Paul's personal weakness was seen in his recent dealings with them as a congregation. We saw in chapter 1 that Paul's relationship with this church spanned several years and was carried out through various means. In the midst of these relations, on one occasion Paul had apparently intended to visit the Corinthians but had changed his mind, opting to avoid visiting Corinth at that time. This seemingly trivial alteration of the apostle's plans was seized on as damning proof of his general instability—and what is more, proof of his lack of devotion to the Corinthians. It seems that his opponents were whispering into the ears of the congregation: "Where is Paul, anyway? He doesn't seem to care about us—see how he's always gone, visiting other churches." Such accusations may lie behind Paul's vehement defense of his change of travel plans: "I intended to come to you before...to pass by way of you to Macedonia, to come again from Macedonia to you.... Moreover I call God as witness against my soul, that to spare you I came no more to Corinth" (2 Cor. 1:15–16, 23). Whether or not they would accept Paul's explanation for this itinerary change—and the spirit in which he made it—would have a direct impact on the future health of their relationship.

Finally, Paul was sharply criticized for not receiving material support from the Corinthians and instead choosing to support himself financially while working among them. At the same time, it appears that his rival pastors had welcomed payment from the Corinthians (2:17). His opponents seem to have claimed that their acceptance of financial support meant that they loved the congregation more than Paul did (11:11). This is a complicated issue, which we will explore in the next chapter. For now, we turn from these various criticisms and complaints to consider Paul's response.

Paul's Response

When a pastor is criticized, it is easy for him to react badly. A natural response is to become angry and resentful, resolving to withhold love from those who voiced the criticism. A second strategy is to become over-defensive by hurrying to list one's good qualities and excellent contributions. And because some congregational members undoubtedly have characters that are negatively inclined or easily displeased, it can also be tempting for the criticized pastor to dismiss almost any words of critique with a flat reminder to "consider the source." In other words, because it came from a Negative Nellie or a Pessimistic Pete, the criticism need not be taken seriously. Another classic response to criticism is the withdrawal or sheltering strategy of putting up emotional walls, lest anyone get close enough to inflict hurt. The pastor holds back with his expressions of pastoral affection in an effort to decrease the possibility of getting stung by future words of criticism.

But Paul's response to criticism in 2 Corinthians is remarkable and bold. Perhaps it is uniquely apostolic, for Paul does not seem to acknowledge any wrongdoing! Yet his response is more than a pretended claim to infallibility. Instead, his whole defense is based on the cross of Christ and on the character of ministry that the cross demands. As Jesus had given Himself unstintingly for the good of His people, so Paul will give himself unreservedly for their spiritual growth. Because of this sacrificial model, he is determined to continue in self-giving love for the Corinthians. He asserts that he has already given much for their pastoral care: "For our boasting is this: the testimony of our conscience that we conducted ourselves in the world in simplicity and godly sincerity, not with fleshly wisdom but by the grace of God, and more abundantly toward you" (1:12). Because of this grace-shaped model of ministry, Paul is willing to continue to be weak and to suffer in the service of the Corinthians. Apparently, he is even willing to endure criticism and opposition, whether it is fair or unfair.

Paul and His Critics

Despite his generally upbeat response to the Corinthian criticism, we can well imagine that Paul felt betrayed by the congregation for how they had sided with his opponents. Certainly he desires that they will see the truth about both them and him; he tells the Corinthians that he wants to "give you opportunity to boast on our behalf, that you may have an answer for those who boast in appearance and not in heart" (5:12). Paul takes a dim view of these other pastors for boasting about such vain things as external appearances. He refers to them as "false" (11:13), and sarcastically describes them as superior to himself (12:11), for they have exalted themselves and taken a position that is not rightly theirs. Yet Paul is even more concerned with the impact of these trying circumstances on the Corinthians, for they have come to harbor reservations about the apostle and his message.

He does admit that it is folly to stoop to the level of his rivals by indulging in boasting. But if it would help the cause of the gospel and move the Corinthians to seek Christ, he will risk sounding like a fool; he asserts, "Seeing that many boast according to the flesh, I also will boast" (11:18). Referring to these other ministers, he first asks, "Are they Hebrews? So am I. Are they Israelites? So am I. Are they the seed of Abraham? So am I" (v. 22). These other pastors claimed to be full-blooded Jews, as if that made them more qualified. But Paul says this gives them no advantage, because he is a Jew just as authentically as they are. Even so, Paul knows that it is a "snare to compare." It is always dangerous to look at what others have and who they are, because you will either be eaten up with envy or become swollen with pride.

Paul could undoubtedly have boasted in personal achievements. To put the Corinthians straight, he just had to send them his résumé. He had established numerous churches around the Roman Empire. He, too, had performed miracles. He had even seen the risen Savior and received visions of inexpressible things. But he will not glory in any of this. He insists, "Of such a one I will boast; yet of myself I will not boast, except in my infirmities" (12:5). Why will he boast in his weaknesses? In order that the attention falls not on him as an apostle and pastor, but on the Lord—on His grace, on His strength, and on His great works!

And so Paul does not recount his various praiseworthy accomplishments. If the rival pastors dared to compare, then they should compare what matters: ministerial sufferings for the sake of the gospel. So he begins to speak of his weakness: "Are they ministers of Christ?—I speak as a fool—I am more: in labors more abundant, in stripes above measure, in prisons more frequently, in deaths often" (11:23). It is as if he says to the Corinthians, "You're right: I *am* weak. I am not glamorous or charismatic like some. I do suffer, almost all the time. I fall short. And I wouldn't want it any other way, because if I was more notable as a person, the gospel might lose its power among you. You would put more confidence in the messenger than in the message—you would start looking at me, not at Christ." Paul is gladly weak, so that God's grace can shine more brightly through him. In short, Paul turns the criticism on its head: if his shortcomings mean that the gospel becomes more prominent, then let him—and every pastor—be a weakling. If his personal failings and inadequacies make the gospel shine more brightly, then let him—and every preacher—fade into the background. So Paul boasts not in churches founded, letters written, converts won, or money collected, but in his sufferings for the cause of Christ.

Lessons from Paul

We have already begun to learn from Pastor Paul some key principles for responding to criticism. It is time to make these lessons more overt. In the first place, it is notable that he does not want others to think too highly of him; he writes, "For though I might desire to boast, I will not be a fool; for I will speak the truth. But I refrain, lest anyone should think of me above what he sees me to be or hears from me" (12:6). This statement is so countercultural that one might think Paul is being disingenuous, but there is no reason to suspect him of insincerity. Within the context of the chapter and letter, it is part of Paul's effort to show himself as weak and inadequate. Though he is seeking to react to his critics and detractors, his concern is not to elevate himself in the view of the Corinthians, but for them to see him rightly so that they will rest more fully in Christ. Paul's fear that someone might think more of him than they ought is precisely the opposite of what we often fear, especially when we are criticized: we *want* to be regarded more highly! But Paul's abiding concern is that sinners look to Christ and not to him. This purpose overrides everything for Paul, even what must have been his natural desire to defend himself or to go on the offensive against his foes. This is a challenging lesson for the criticized pastor: Christ's glory is always more important than our own prestige, and His honor always more crucial than our own reputation.

A second key truth in Paul's response to his critics is that he conducts his ministry in the sight of God. In various places in 2 Corinthians, he expressly sets himself before God's judgment and evaluation. For instance, when defending his practice of self-support, he asks the question, "Because I do not love you? *God knows!*" (11:11). And in the following chapter, he asserts, "We speak *before God* in Christ" (12:19). His keen awareness of ministering under God's watchfulness and judgment means that he is not overly concerned with the judgments of other people. He will respond to his critics in Corinth for the sake of the gospel's truth, but his focus is on pleasing the Lord above all. As he wrote in 1 Corinthians, "For I know of nothing against myself, yet I am not justified by this; *but He who judges me is the Lord*" (4:4). Infinitely weightier than human opinions is God's evaluation. This realization was freeing to Paul, and it can also liberate the criticized pastor today as he commits his work to God in prayer. Criticism is hard to receive—and unfounded criticism is particularly discouraging and frustrating—but a pastor does his task firstly before the Lord and primarily under His scrutiny. On account of inborn pride and the desire to boast in human accomplishments, this is a difficult truth to accept, yet it is surely the key to God's blessing: remembering at all times that you serve Christ and must give an account to Him.

While it is striking that Paul does not seem to admit wrongdoing in this letter, he is surely aware of his shortcomings. This is a third lesson, and one that is sobering: no pastor's work is without flaw. As human beings, we are weak, inconsistent, and unwise, and so we will receive criticism. The apostle Paul did, and even the Lord Jesus did! Perhaps it is true that some congregational members take notice only when a poor, deficient, or not-to-their-expectations job is done, and they offer little commendation for all the good and faithful work that has been done. Not everyone will appreciate the pastor, or say that they do. Nonetheless, a pastor should learn not to need praise and affirmation after every sermon, even though he might be proud of each one, and though he might have spent laborious hours on each one. Indeed, a pastor can never claim that he doesn't need to learn or grow, for every servant of Christ needs reflection, correction, and reorientation in his holy task. Thus when criticism is received—even from someone in the congregation who has taken on the role of "critic"—it is right that a pastor accepts this as a God-given means to growth. Reading 2 Corinthians, one gets the sense that Paul had been granted an excellent opportunity to grow through the strain and stress of his relationship with the Corinthians. Indeed, it was through this conflict and controversy that Paul developed his insights into the true character and focus of Christian ministry. For a pastor today, criticism can be lovingly used by God to sanctify, teach, and mature His servants.

Collecting Compliments

The same arrogance that prevents us from receiving criticism well also leads us to eagerly receive compliments. To be sure, it is good when God uses congregational members to confirm and encourage the minister in his task. For example, it is helpful for a pastor to know that his Sunday sermons are communicating faithfully and effectively. However, a pastor may also be tempted to become boastful when he considers his advanced education, skills, longevity, and various successes in ministry. These may be things for which he thinks he ought to garner some recognition. And so when there is a chorus of congregational praise for his good efforts or abilities, pride is lurking, together with a disturbing ingratitude toward God. A pastor might have prayed for something sincerely, asking God at the beginning of the week for wisdom, endurance, or boldness, but later applauds *himself*: "It was a successful sermon, thanks to my wise exegesis and sound delivery. From what the congregation said, it was my passion and charisma that really carried the worship along today." God might get mentioned in the footnote, but the pastor is the main character. It is little wonder that Proverbs teaches this wisdom: "The refining pot is for silver and the furnace for gold, and a man is valued by what others say of him" (27:21). Pastors—and all people—are tested by praise. What does it reveal about us? Are we walking in pride or humility? Are we filled with gratitude to God or arrogance?

Because other people's praise feeds our pride, compliments can become addictive. Commended once for a strong sermon, celebrated twice for his approachability, a pastor can find himself always needing to hear more. The desire for praise is never satisfied, and it is a most unpleasant hunger. Compounding this problem is the changeability of our own moods. A pastor might learn that the feeling of being appreciated is hopelessly subjective. He can feel greatly loved and cherished for a few weeks, basing this sense on little more than a handful of positive comments. Conversely, a couple of months later he might feel utterly taken for granted and undervalued by the congregation, as there has been so little vocal appreciation recently. The fact is, if a pastor is listening for compliments, he will hear them; if he is listening for criticism, he will hear that, too, whether or not either is intended. Again, the approval of others can be a desperate idol, where a person is always hungry for more offerings of praise, compliments, and recognition—but is never satisfied. So a pastor ought to learn to perform his work for God above all: "He who judges me is the Lord" (1 Cor. 4:4).

With his radically countercultural words, Paul teaches that pastors should never want to be thought of more highly than is warranted. Jeremiah teaches the same lesson when he says that the people of Israel needed to boast in something more than having received circumcision or being scrupulous in outward religion:

Thus says the LORD:

"Let not the wise man glory in his wisdom,
Let not the mighty man glory in his might,
Nor let the rich man glory in his riches;
But let him who glories glory in this,
That he understands and knows Me,
That I am the LORD, exercising lovingkindness, judgment,
   and righteousness in the earth.
For in these I delight," says the LORD. (Jer. 9:23–24)

Instead of putting stock in worldly wisdom, personal charm, and
human strength, and instead of equating compliments with ministerial success, Jeremiah and Paul remind us of the only thing in which
redeemed sinners—and that includes pastors!—should glory: that
we know the Lord and rest completely in His power. In this spirit,
a pastor also ought to be willing to rejoice in the successes of other
pastors. Rather than be stirred by a worldly spirit of jealousy or a
competitive urge when he sees ministerial colleagues do well, he can
be quietly grateful that God is working powerfully among His people. Paul's words in 1 Corinthians 3:7 are suitably humbling for every
pastor and preacher, "So then neither he who plants is anything, nor
he who waters, but God who gives the increase." We need to realize
that it is only through Christ that we can serve Christ in order to
advance His church.

All-Sufficient Grace

Human weakness has a marvelous way of revealing God's strength.
When we finally stop focusing on what we can accomplish, it is then
that God's grace becomes most visible. When we finally acknowledge that we cannot do it by ourselves, God shows his presence in
new and surprising ways. This is also true for a pastor, that when he
finally admits his limitations and acknowledges that he is far from
perfect, Christ will make him a strong and effective servant. As
Christ said to Paul, "My grace is sufficient for you, for My strength
is made perfect in weakness" (2 Cor. 12:9). This truth is essential to
embrace, because there should be many moments when a pastor

realizes how inadequate he is, just how little he knows, and that he really has no idea what to do or say next.

Looking back on the years of ministry, a pastor will see that a multitude of mistakes were made. Criticism simply puts these things into focus more clearly. Sermons were flubbed. People were rightly offended. There were bloopers, slipups, and there were many faux pas. Worst of all, a pastor knows how far he was personally from meeting the holy standard of God's Word, the same Scriptures that he was privileged to preach every Sunday. But if a weak pastor humbles himself and remembers that effective ministry is not dependent on his interpersonal abilities, his wise and persuasive words, or his own holiness, then the strong Christ will lift him up with all-sufficient grace. When a pastor admits that his work is about glorifying Christ and not defending or promoting himself, he will be able to carry on in good courage and new purpose.

Every weak servant of Christ can cling to the ancient words of Zechariah 4:6, "'Not by might nor by power, but by My Spirit,' says the LORD of hosts." These are God's words to Zerubbabel the priest as he led the people through the trying time of rebuilding a ruined temple. Military strength or human ingenuity would not be the key to accomplishing their daunting project, but the Israelites had to depend entirely on the Spirit of the almighty God. These words are still a much-needed message about whose strength is absolutely essential for being a preacher and pastor. When they are filled with a proud spirit of self-reliance and overconfidence, pastors need this humbling reminder. Likewise, when they have been deflated again by criticism and a keen sense of their own weakness, pastors can derive much strength from this sure promise of God: "You will do it by My Spirit." This is where the power is for every imperfect pastor—so it has always been, and will always be.

CHAPTER 6

HANDLING MONEY WISELY

*I robbed other churches, taking wages
from them to minister to you.*
—2 CORINTHIANS 11:8

There was a precise moment when I first realized that a pastor's pay was a matter for public discussion. It was years ago in my first congregation, and I was leading an annual general meeting with the church members. Such a meeting was an occasion for the congregation to be updated on various initiatives from the board of elders, the work being done by the church committees, and recent projects of mission and mercy. Part of the meeting was also spent reviewing the congregation's budget for the upcoming year: expected revenue (mostly through voluntary contributions) and anticipated expenses (such as building maintenance and mission contributions). Of course, one of the church's budgeted expenses was the financial support for the pastor, namely, me. And when I later gave the opportunity for any questions from the floor, an older brother stood up and voiced his opinion that I should receive an immediate and substantial raise! His reasoning was that because I had studied for eight years—about as long as a lawyer or a medical doctor—my pay should be roughly on par with those professions. Thus he proposed to the meeting that I receive a pay raise of not less than $20,000 per year. I will admit that it was hard to suppress a smile and to act disinterested. Thankfully, one of the church's elders intervened to address the question in a tactful way. And while the comment was well-intended, it did make for an awkward moment: a public discussion of how much money I should be paid, with me present. It was a small glimpse into some of the complications surrounding the question of pastoral pay, complications that Paul had to carefully navigate in his relationship with the Corinthians.

A Congregation with Giving Potential

In an earlier chapter we saw that Corinth was a prosperous mercantile city, and as such it was a prime place for Paul to earn money through his manual trade. According to Acts 18:1–3, Paul worked as a tentmaker in the eighteen months he was ministering in Corinth, and the city's bustling economy meant that he (working together with Aquila and Priscilla) probably would have enjoyed a steady stream of business. However, it is precisely this self-support and its social implications that became a contentious issue between Paul and the Corinthians.

There are actually two issues related to money in 2 Corinthians: support for needy churches and support for Paul's ministry. To set the stage for our focus on the second matter, we will briefly outline the first issue. In the early years of the church, there was a lot of concern for the believers who were living in Jerusalem and Judea. In the book of Acts, we read about a severe famine that was expected to afflict the Roman Empire and particularly the area of Palestine (11:28). This natural disaster, combined with sporadic persecutions, resulted in the Judean Christians suffering badly. They needed financial help for an extended period of time. Acts recounts how Paul worked to mobilize churches throughout the empire to support their needy brothers and sisters in Judea (e.g., 11:29–30). Because they enjoyed a unity in faith, the gentiles knew that they could not be idle while their brothers and sisters in Christ experienced serious need. Instead, generous giving across racial and cultural lines would be a powerful expression of oneness in Christ (see Rom. 15:25–27).

Already in 1 Corinthians, Paul promoted a spirit of charity toward the needy. He instructed the congregation, "On the first day of the week let each one of you lay something aside, storing up as he may prosper, that there be no collections when I come" (1 Cor. 16:2). As he did with other churches, Paul had called the Corinthians to diligently show generosity to the poor. But his words were not received as enthusiastically as he would have liked. For by the time of 2 Corinthians, it seems that progress in the collection has begun to stall, and Paul must urge them to give more liberally. He begins this part of his letter (chapters 8–9) by mentioning the Macedonian churches: "We make known to you the grace of God bestowed on the churches of Macedonia: that in a great trial of affliction the abundance of their joy and their deep poverty abounded in the riches of their liberality" (2 Cor. 8:1–2). It seems as if Paul is applying some positive peer pressure to the Corinthians, pointing to their Macedonian neighbors who themselves struggled financially, but who gave according to their ability, "yes, and beyond their ability" (v. 3).

Now Paul wants the Corinthians to imitate them by being cheerful givers. He promises that God will surely bless those who are generous, while he also warns against the results of sowing sparingly (cf. 9:6). But with these exhortations Paul has a steep hill to climb, probably because of the current strain on his relationship with the Corinthians. For together with their various criticisms of Paul, there went an apparent reluctance to answer his appeal for famine relief. The Corinthians had previously been willing to give, but it seems that they have now begun to close their hearts and wallets. For this reason, Paul urges them to complete what they started (8:11), and he calls them to follow through on their good intentions in thankfulness for God's grace in Christ (v. 9). His hope is that their renewed giving for the needs of the saints will be "a matter of generosity and not as a grudging obligation" (9:5). With God's blessing, the Corinthians would be a people who exercised their full potential for giving.

Paul's Pattern of Self-Support

Even as Paul exhorts the Corinthians to give generously to support the poor, he needs to address why he has not accepted their financial contributions toward his own work of ministry. In examining this issue, we should be reminded of the general pattern of Paul's ministry. While he would remain in a given location to work for as long as three years, his intention was always to move on to new areas in which to spread the gospel (Rom. 15:20). And whenever he arrived in a new region or city, Paul needed to consider his personal upkeep. How would he cover the costs of his food, accommodations, and any other daily expenses? In the time of the Roman Empire, there were generally four means of material support available to itinerant teachers like Paul: one could charge fees from the audience, beg for financial assistance, work in self-support, or seek the help of a wealthy patron or sponsor.

In general, Paul tried to maintain financial independence when he was working among the churches. His parting words to the Ephesian elders in Acts 20:33–34 are revealing of his practice: "I have coveted no one's silver or gold or apparel. Yes, you yourselves know that these hands have provided for my necessities, and for those who were with me." He wrote similarly to the Thessalonians, "You remember, brethren, our labor and toil; for laboring night and day, that we might not be a burden to any of you, we preached to you the gospel of God" (1 Thess. 2:9; cf. 2 Thess. 3:7–9). In many cities—not just in Corinth—this had been his normal practice: to perform his tentmaking trade alongside the work of his ministry so that he did not need to depend on the material support of those to whom he preached.

Yet it must be pointed out that Paul was also willing to accept assistance from some congregations. For instance, to the Philippians he expresses a warm gratitude for their financial support (Phil. 4:10, 15). And their generosity was not limited to his time of working among them: "Even in Thessalonica you sent aid once and again for my necessities" (v. 16). To accept such support was wholly legitimate, for Paul considered that this was one of his God-ordained rights as an apostle. He had previously explained to the Corinthians,

Or is it only Barnabas and I who have no right to refrain from working? Who ever goes to war at his own expense? Who plants a vineyard and does not eat of its fruit? Or who tends a flock and does not drink of the milk of the flock?

Do I say these things as a mere man? Or does not the law say the same also? For it is written in the law of Moses, "You shall not muzzle an ox while it treads out the grain." Is it oxen God is concerned about? Or does He say it altogether for our sakes? For our sakes, no doubt, this is written, that he who plows should plow in hope, and he who threshes in hope should be partaker of his hope. If we have sown spiritual things for you, is it a great thing if we reap your material things? If others are partakers of this right over you, are we not even more? (1 Cor. 9:6–12)

In this passage Paul does not simply give a pragmatic rationale, but he bases the practice of a congregation supporting its pastor on the principles of the Old Testament law. For instance, Deuteronomy 25:4 stipulated that even oxen were permitted to enjoy some of the fruits of their labor while they treaded out the grain. What is more, Paul points out, "Even so the Lord has commanded that those who preach the gospel should live from the gospel" (1 Cor. 9:14). Paul here is likely referring to the teaching of Jesus when he instructs his disciples to enjoy the hospitality of those who are willing to receive their preaching: "And remain in the same house, eating and drinking such things as they give, for the laborer is worthy of his wages" (Luke 10:7). If Paul or any other pastor requested and accepted financial assistance from a local congregation, such a practice had support that was indubitably well-founded.

The Corinthians' Criticism

Paul had spoken to the Corinthians about "reaping material things" from his spiritual labors among them, yet he had acknowledged in the same breath, "Nevertheless we have not used this right, but endure all things lest we hinder the gospel of Christ" (1 Cor. 9:12). We have seen that during his initial stay in Corinth, Paul worked with his hands to support himself (Acts 18:1–3). On his subsequent visits to Corinth he must also have turned down the financial assistance of the congregation, preaching "free of charge" (2 Cor. 11:7). This refusal of payment was condemned as being offensive to the congregation and had become badly detrimental to Paul's relationship with them. His ironic question reveals the tensions simmering around this issue: "Did I commit sin in humbling myself that you might be exalted, because I preached the gospel of God to you free of charge?" (v. 7).

Now, it is difficult for a twenty-first-century reader to appreciate fully the gravity of these circumstances. I suspect that most churches today would be happy to remove "pastor's pay" from the annual church budget if their pastor had found a sustainable (and legal) way to support himself while continuing to work full-time in the congregation! We struggle to understand what the problem with Paul's self-support really was, yet many in Corinth severely criticized him for his stance on this matter.

When we consider the cultural background of the Corinthians, we see a first possible reason why Paul's self-support became a divisive issue. In the eyes of some people, Paul was akin to the traveling orators who frequently came to their city seeking opportunity to lecture in front of a paying audience. Such traveling teachers were often evaluated by the amount of money they earned. With many itinerant instructors in religion and philosophy moving through the cities and towns of the empire, the field was highly competitive. A good teacher could earn well and thereby enhance his reputation. At the same time, people liked to brag about how much money they were paying their resident teacher. Higher pay meant better quality, which in turn meant a superior audience. So for Paul to teach and preach for free suggested that he was little more than a second-rate speaker, while those who listened to him were obviously undiscerning about the quality of the message they heard. Paul's self-support reflected badly not only on him but also on them.

A second reason that Paul's self-support was criticized may have been rooted in a disdain for manual labor. In the words of the Roman statesman and philosopher Cicero, "Unbecoming to a gentleman...

and vulgar are the means of livelihood of all hired workmen whom we pay for mere manual labour, not for artistic skill; for in their case the very wage they receive is a pledge of their slavery" (*On Duties*, trans. W. Miller, 1.150). It would be consistent with this view that some of the socially pretentious Corinthians looked down on people who worked with their hands. While Jewish rabbis usually had a trade, Greco-Roman teachers did not, for it was considered degrading and improper. Consequently, the Corinthians may have been ashamed that one of their spiritual leaders had stooped to the lowly position of the work of a tentmaker.

Although Paul declined to receive the Corinthians' material support for his ministry, we have seen that he did ask for money in order to support the needy churches of Judea (2 Corinthians 8–9). This request is at the heart of a third possible reason that the Corinthians criticized Paul: they may have been suspicious that he was actually collecting the funds for himself. In other words, he was defrauding the Corinthians while pretending to have a materially disinterested attitude. This suspicion is reflected in Paul's words of self-defense in chapter 12. After affirming to the Corinthians that he did not seek their possessions but was ready to "be spent for your souls" (v. 15), he asks, "Did I take advantage of you?" (v. 17). Likewise, he insists in 2 Corinthians 7:2, "We have cheated no one." Paul here may be denying the accusation that he had exploited them in taking their money, supposedly for famine relief but actually for enriching himself.

While each of these factors could be part of the criticism of Paul's self-support, there is another, more likely reason, one rooted in the Greco-Roman customs of patronage and friendship. The key dynamic in patronage was based on the power and influence that went along with the giving of gifts. In short, the recipient of any gift was considered to owe both gratitude and public honor to the giver. Thus, while the giving of a gift certainly helped the recipient, it served to improve the social status of the donor or patron at the same time. Those who exploited this power recognized that other people could be placed in their debt by giving them some benefit. The social obligation on the recipient was so great that a failure to reciprocate was considered a rejection of friendship and reasonable grounds for enmity. If a relationship was going to be properly maintained, there had to be a mutual expression of liberality and loyalty: the classic quid pro quo.

Viewed in this context, Paul's refusal of the Corinthians' financial support was no trifling matter. To decline their patronage was widely criticized by the socially minded Corinthians. His opponents interpreted Paul's financial independence as an affront to the congregation; his refusal of help was indicative of a lack of love and a rejection of their friendship (11:7–11). Compounding the problem for Paul's relationship with this church was that he had accepted financial aid from the Philippians, but not the Corinthians—an inconsistency on Paul's part and a sure proof of his lack of affection. Indeed, his rivals alleged that Paul turned down their support because he considered them to be inferior to other congregations (12:13). With his acceptance of payment from one church and not from another, the Corinthians considered that Paul was to blame for the deterioration of their relationship.

Paul's Defense

If it was such an obviously contentious matter, why did Paul turn down the material support of the Corinthians? And why does he insist that he will continue this practice despite their caustic complaints (11:12)? In the first place, Paul probably sought to distance himself from his rivals who charged people to listen to their polished oratory. As we saw in a previous chapter, he did not want to be associated with those who were "peddling the word of God" (2:17). By his self-support, Paul would "cut off the opportunity from those who desire an opportunity to be regarded just as we are in the things of which they boast" (11:12). He instead considered it a demonstration of his genuine love for the congregation to preach "free of charge." Thus, if his rivals would not preach gratis as Paul did, then the congregation should view them with suspicion because of their greed, and should certainly not consider Paul to be inferior to them.

Another probable reason that Paul turned down offers of support was his wish to remain free of personal obligations to any patrons. This impartiality was essential in a church that had been as fragmented as Corinth, where there were congregational groups who were loyal to one leader over against another (cf. 1 Cor. 1:10–13). To have accepted the patronage of certain individuals would have placed Paul in a situation of personal loyalty to one or more members of the church. This would have hampered his efforts to pastor the congregation as a whole effectively. In short, Paul knows that if he accepts their money, the cause of the gospel in Corinth will be harmed. The gospel should be freely available to all so that there is no hindrance to hearing and accepting Christ's message.

Interestingly, however, Paul gives no explicit reason for his refusal of support. The nearest that he comes is to declare that as the Corinthians' spiritual father, he is materially responsible for them. Appealing to the accepted notion that parents ought to provide for their children, he insists in 2 Corinthians 12:14, "And I will not be burdensome to you; for I do not seek yours, but you. For the children ought not to lay up for the parents, but the parents for the children." Paul saw his refusal of their financial aid as consistent with his "parental duties," carried out for their benefit. Through his self-sacrificing ministry, he is focused on promoting the Corinthians' spiritual well-being rather than in acquiring their material possessions for himself. In all this, Paul is definitely not seeking to be free of his obligations toward the Corinthians. Instead, what he desires is a reciprocal and open relationship, where he can speak candidly to his children and where they will respond to their father with expressions of genuine honor and love (cf. 6:11–12).

Viewing self-support as a component of Paul's model for ministry, it stands as yet another demonstration of his self-giving love for the churches. Wanting to prove his commitment to the Corinthians and not discredit the gospel or hamper his ministry within this congregation, Paul is willing to forgo one of his rights as an apostle. It was no doubt a demanding task at which Paul worked in tentmaking, but in 1 Corinthians 4:11–12 he counts it among the many struggles that he is willing to endure for the good of the church: "To the present hour we both hunger and thirst, and we are poorly clothed, and beaten, and homeless. *And we labor, working with our own hands.*" Such a decision to support himself cost Paul dearly in terms of time, effort, and misunderstanding, yet it was a precious display of his pastoral affection. It is consistent with how he depicts his ministry in 2 Corinthians 6:10, "as poor, yet making many rich; as having nothing, and yet possessing all things." By Paul's poverty and suffering, he will seek to enrich the Corinthians, even as his own loss of status allowed him to model the free gift of the gospel. The next chapter will show that it is entirely consistent with Christ's gospel that his pastors are humble and willing to be abased.

Financial Lessons for Today

What lessons can we learn from Paul's approach to the financial support of his ministry? We should be mindful that cultural dynamics have changed considerably since the first-century Greco-Roman world. For instance, issues surrounding patrons and patronage are likely no longer a concern for contemporary pastors. Yet there are analogous tensions surrounding financial support today, and there are important scriptural principles that remain relevant for pastors and churches alike. I will draw out five applicable lessons on this topic from 2 Corinthians.

1. God commands the church to materially support the gospel ministry.
It is a New Testament principle that those who receive the benefits of the gospel ministry must be willing to support its workers. This principle is abundantly clear from Paul's teachings in places such as Acts 20:33–34; 1 Thessalonians 2:9; and 2 Thessalonians 3:7–9. We have seen that even as Paul declines financial support from the Corinthians, he insists that it is his God-given right to receive payment for his work of ministry. Rooting this practice in Old Testament patterns of support for the priests and Levites working at the temple, he says, "Do you not know that those who minister the holy things eat of the things of the temple, and those who serve at the altar partake

of the offerings of the altar? Even so the Lord has commanded that those who preach the gospel should live from the gospel" (1 Cor. 9:13–14). In a similar way, Jesus instructed His disciples to receive hospitality from those to whom they preached, and He affirmed that "the laborer is worthy of his wages" (Luke 10:7). Notably, Jesus appeals to something that is already known from the sphere of ordinary labor and He applies it to ministry labor. He does not merely say, "Accept payment because ministry deserves it," but Jesus reasons that just as laborers in every other context deserve their proper wages, so do those who labor in the Lord's church.

It is therefore incumbent on a church to faithfully support the gospel ministry as it is carried out in their midst. To be sure, this support will take on different forms depending on the possibilities of the local context. Some pastors will need to have a "tentmaking" ministry, as Paul did, literally. That is, when a local congregation is unable to support its pastor fully, he might need to take on some other paid labor for material support. I've been told that in earlier times of my own denomination, when most families were recent immigrants and not financially well-established, church members would drop off baskets of apples and trays of eggs at the minister's door, or maybe a quarter of a cow or pig for the freezer. Today, ministers might receive an automatic deposit into their bank account every month, a house to live in, and even a vehicle to drive. As Jesus says, gospel laborers are worthy of such support. What is more, this support allows pastors to allocate more of their time each week—or all of their time—to the demanding tasks of ministry, without being distracted by material cares or occupied with paid labors that are unrelated to ministry.

Jesus's words to His disciples in Luke 22:36 acknowledge that in some difficult situations, such as in times of persecution, a minister will need to support himself: "But now, he who has a money bag, let him take it." Likewise, missionaries today generally do not expect to be supported by the people to whom they preach the gospel, at least initially. Later, as new believers mature in the faith and in their understanding of the Scriptures, they can be taught to give freely for the gospel ministry. Support for the ministry looks different in different places and situations, but in general the principle remains: through their grateful giving, church members should support those who work in the gospel so that Christ's gospel can continue to be preached.

2. A pastor should not be focused on financially profiting from his work.

Paul was acutely aware of the corrupting influence that money can have on a pastor's ministry, whether through the enslavement of greed or the manipulation of the message. This is clear in Paul's insistence to the Ephesian elders that while he was among them he "coveted no one's silver or gold" (Acts 20:33), and it is also clear in his denunciation of those who peddle the Word of God for personal profit (2 Cor. 2:17). This temptation remains real for those in ministry today. Perhaps a pastor is lured to take a position at a church that offers to pay substantially more than his present congregation. Or perhaps a pastor is quick to complain that he needs a raise in his salary, or he always seeks to maximize every financial benefit that is available to him. But here a pastor must tread carefully. Even the appearance of being focused on financially profiting from ministry can be detrimental to his relationship with the congregation, and it can hinder the believers' growth in Christ. Paul's words to the Corinthians are a good reminder of what must take priority: "I do not seek yours"—that is, the Corinthians' material possessions—"but *you*" (2 Cor. 12:14). What a faithful pastor seeks is not his own material gain, but the congregation's continued and fruitful walk with Christ.

The challenge for pastors in this regard is the same challenge that is faced by all Christians. By nature we want to stand on our rights, insist on recognition and honor, and maintain our entitlements. Yet Scripture exhorts all believers to be content with what we have (1 Tim. 6:6). As people who have been saved by Jesus and who have freely received God's costly gift of redemption, we have the greatest reason to be content. Not only is this so, but God the Father has also promised to supply all our daily needs. As Hebrews 13:5 says, "Let your conduct be without covetousness; be content with such things as you have. For He himself has said, 'I will never leave you nor forsake you.'" With confidence in God's sure promise, pastors ought to keep the focus where it needs to be: doing the work of dedicated ministry among Christ's people and trusting in God to provide the requisite material things. Such a contented approach to money will set a good example to the congregation and will also honor Christ and His gospel.

3. Churches and pastors should aim for transparency in financial matters relating to the ministry.

Reviewing the two letters to the Corinthians, one is struck by the amount of attention that Paul devotes to financial matters. As we have seen, in 1 and 2 Corinthians he explains his right to their material support, clarifies that he will not be receiving it from the congregation, and at length exhorts the church to keep contributing for famine relief. He even discloses that he has accepted money from other congregations, but not from the Corinthians. This deliberate consideration of monetary matters undoubtedly arises out of Paul's desire for openness and clarity about a topic that has always had dangerous and divisive potential among God's people. In other places in his letters (e.g., 1 Tim. 6:6–10, 17), Paul echoes the words of Jesus about the corrupting power of the love of money (e.g., Luke 12:13–21). And because a love of money can unduly sway a pastor's teaching or even ruin his ministry, it is necessary that churches and pastors alike recognize the need for being wholly transparent in financial matters relating to the work of ministry. Pastors must be above reproach in how they handle money, while churches should be sensitive to the ways in which money matters can expose a spiritual ugliness in the character of both pastors and their congregants.

At the beginning of this chapter, I shared a story about the kind of uncomfortable conversation that can take place when the pastor's pay is a subject for public discussion. Although it was awkward, I would not want it any other way, particularly because of the importance of a church's leaders being transparent and open about financial matters that pertain to themselves. It is wise to show "the numbers" to the congregation and invite their questions and comments. To be sure, there are ways to conduct such a discussion in a sensible and circumspect manner. For instance, a public meeting is not an appropriate forum for reviewing the pastor's "performance" and making comments on his current levels of remuneration relative to such a review. A review of the pastor's work can take place in a consultative manner without being entirely public. Likewise, at public meetings it is prudent to have an unpaid representative from the board of elders field any questions about the pay of church employees. However it is done, prioritizing transparency is a simple way to protect the integrity of pastors and to preserve the unity of the congregation.

4. A pastor should be aware of the possible influences and pressures from donors.

In declining the Corinthians' material support, Paul was sensitive to the social obligations under which receiving payment would place him. There may well have been a pressure on him to adapt his preaching to suit the wishes and preferences of the Corinthians. And so Paul insisted on being free from their constraints so that he could bring the gospel according to his Spirit-led conviction. In our time and culture, the interpersonal dynamics and pressures of patronage have faded, but there may be attempts to influence a pastor through the giving of gifts or other favors. Like any public figure in leadership, a minister of the gospel should be wary of conflicts of interest, real or perceived. Because a pastor has a higher profile than most people in the congregation, some church members may wish to foster a special relationship with the pastor. Such a close relationship may bring the benefit of improved (or imagined) social prestige or the opportunity to sway the pastor's viewpoints on various matters. Furthermore, a pastor is preaching to the same people who contribute funds to his monthly salary, a reality that can give rise to the temptation to try to avoid stepping on any proverbial toes in the Sunday sermons. Better to play it safe with another affirming, vanilla-flavored sermon, than to risk a decrease in contributions toward the budget!

All of this means that a pastor should be aware of the pressures that may be exerted on him by those in the congregation who are wealthy or who seek to give special gifts to the minister. There should be no sense of obligation to people because of their long history of financial support or because of their position in the congregation; a pastor should do his work before God without favoritism or partiality. Now, this is not to say that a pastor should be suspicious of every act of kindness or generosity shown toward him and his family. In my years of pastoral ministry, my family and I have been greatly blessed by our congregations through many thoughtful gifts, bouquets of flowers, superb dinners, and special opportunities, such as boat rides and city outings. For those who love Christ and His gospel, a generous treatment of the minister of the Word can be considered a fitting way to show appreciation. Nevertheless, our hearts are still stubbornly prone to be self-seeking and oriented toward personal benefit, even when doing good works for Christ, whether giving material gifts or preaching the gospel. Pastors and congregational members alike are subject to this weakness, and so we must all beware of how good works should not be done for our own gain but for the glory of God.

5. In financial matters, the cause of the gospel must always take the primary place.

Throughout our study of 2 Corinthians so far, we have seen that Paul has a razor-sharp focus on advancing the cause of the gospel, even at great personal cost to himself. This chapter has revealed that this focus is also evident through Paul's approach to material support. While laboring in Corinth, he decided to support himself so that he could present the gospel "free of charge." Released from the pressures of patronage and insulated from the accusations of greed, Paul could preach the gospel and pastor the congregation in a way that truly served their growth in Christ. Any pastor should be similarly motivated, not wanting to do anything in financial matters that will hinder the cause of the gospel. This means, as we saw above, that a pastor should be eager to promote such things as transparency and open communication in the discussions that relate to his material support. This means also that a pastor may be willing to accept lower pay than expected (given his training or his experience), or that he may be willing to take on some responsibility for self-support, in order that the ministry of the gospel can continue unhindered in a particular place. As far as it depends on the pastor, financial matters should never be allowed to damage or detract from a good and upbuilding relationship with the congregation. In short, the congregants need to know that their pastor loves them more than their money. In this way the cause of Christ's gospel will be promoted.

CHAPTER 7

SUFFERING WILLINGLY

I am exceedingly joyful in all our tribulation.
—2 CORINTHIANS 7:4

Churches can go through periods of being without a pastor. It generally means that a search committee gets formed to find a new man for the job. And when such a committee does its work, they are looking for *strengths*. They want to know if this seminary graduate or that pastor has strength in preaching, counseling, administration, or some other discipline deemed important for ministry in that setting. No committee or board of elders will conclude, "What we really need for our congregation is someone *weak*. A weak preacher, a weak pastor—just a weak character all around is what we're after." Such a proposition you would never hear.

So it is a wonder that the weak Paul had any success as a pastor, and it is a marvel that he survived three or four decades of working in the churches and even seemed effective in his work. It is surprising, particularly considering how he describes his work in 2 Corinthians. From the first chapter to the last he draws attention to his afflictions and weaknesses. For Paul, this is not a reason for shame or regret. He attests that he is happy to be lacking in ability, even boasts about his weakness, and rejoices in his suffering. In this chapter we will unpack what it means for Paul (and any pastor) to be weak and afflicted while resting in the strong Christ.

The Cruciform Model of Ministry

Central to Paul's model of ministry is the truth that Christ's sufferings are perpetuated among His servants as they carry on His work. This is consistent with what Jesus says in Matthew 10:24–25 about how His loyal followers will share in His fate in being persecuted: "A disciple is not above his teacher, nor a servant above his master. It is enough for a disciple that he be like his teacher, and a servant like his master." In the same spirit, Paul explains that he (and other faithful pastors) are "always carrying about in the body the dying of the Lord Jesus, that the life of Jesus also may be manifested in our body. For we who live are always delivered to death for Jesus' sake, that the life of Jesus also may be manifested in our mortal flesh. So then death is working in us, but life in you" (2 Cor. 4:10–12). Here it is clear that Paul regards all ministerial sufferings as a necessary participation in the sufferings of Christ, as the "dying" of the Lord Jesus is put on display through pastoral hardship. In loving his congregations at great cost to himself, Paul affirms that he is aiming to live out the implications of the crucifixion. This is the cruciform model of ministry: performing self-sacrificial service for the good of Christ's people and for the glory of Christ's name. To put it another way, there must be an unbreakable connection between Christology and pastoral theology. For this fundamental reason Paul is willing to endure persecutions and sufferings for the sake of the church, even if these hardships result in his own demise.

It is essential to understand that for Paul, hardship is not a peripheral aspect of his ministry but integral. Not only in 2 Corinthians 4:10–12 but in several other passages of this letter, he speaks of ministry in terms of unity with the suffering Christ. For instance, Paul says that "the sufferings of Christ abound in [him]" when he endures afflictions for the "consolation and salvation" of the believers (1:5–6). Just as Christ suffered in order to bring eternal blessing to His people, so Paul suffers for the spiritual benefit of the churches. We find this theme in his other letters, too, such as in Colossians 1:24, where Paul states, "I now rejoice in my sufferings for you, and fill up in my flesh what is lacking in the afflictions of Christ, for the sake of

His body, which is the church." While there was certainly nothing deficient about His saving work on the cross, the ascended Christ deems it necessary that His servants suffer and struggle in order to advance the gospel and build up His body on earth. Far from being a series of unfortunate events in an otherwise stellar career, Paul's many adversities find their glorious rationale in the reality of Jesus's suffering and death (cf. Gal. 6:14; Phil. 2:17; 2 Tim. 2:10).

Near the end of 2 Corinthians Paul reiterates the basis of his cruciform model of ministry: "For though He was crucified in weakness, yet He lives by the power of God. For we also are weak in Him, but we shall live with Him by the power of God toward you" (2 Cor. 13:4). Paul is willing to admit that he is weak—indeed, he will even boast about it—because it was in weakness that Jesus Himself carried out life-changing service for others. Jesus was not a glamorous and charismatic persona, but a humble teacher from Nazareth. Throughout His ministry, Jesus was greatly affected by the pains of His people around Him. As He told His disciples in Mark 10:45, "For even the Son of Man did not come to be served, but to serve, and to give His life a ransom for many." His first purpose in coming to earth was not to be recognized as notable and glorious, but to be lowly in helping those unable to help themselves. And after struggling throughout His earthly years with the frailties and limitations of the flesh, His life ended with the shame of the cross. "He was crucified in weakness" (2 Cor. 13:4), ostensibly incapable of preventing this from happening and preserving His own life. As Paul has said, the cross is the ultimate statement of weakness and folly (1 Cor. 1:18–24), yet God manifested His power through it by raising Jesus from the dead and saving a world of sinners.

From the definitive example of Jesus's suffering Paul draws a direct line to his own weakness and hardship. Just as Jesus had offered Himself on the cross to accomplish redemption, so Paul seeks to be unashamedly devoted in his labors for the good of the churches. In this letter he attests that he has always tried to demonstrate a cruciform model in his ministry among the Corinthians, working in a manner that is consistent with Jesus's message. As a pastor, Paul will imitate Christ in care and compassion: Jesus was weak, so he can be weak; Jesus gave Himself to serve others, so Paul will do the same.

An Uncomfortable Model

When we consider Paul's high view of a Christlike ministry, we can understand his intensity in defending it throughout this letter. He saw that the Corinthians' contempt for all notions of weakness and suffering actually struck at the heart of the gospel, for their views of church and ministry were far from "cross-shaped." His boasting in weakness and hardships, it is almost needless to say, ran directly counter to the values of the Corinthians. This was a city that championed social climbing, so his deliberate self-abasement would have been deemed offensive. But their preference for an outwardly extraordinary ministry meant that more than Paul's personal honor was at stake—it was the integrity of the church's teaching and preaching. If the status and presentation of the earthly messenger are so important, the actual message may be twisted or neglected. This explains Paul's dismayed words about the destructive work of his rivals in preaching "another Jesus" or sharing "a different gospel": "For if he who comes preaches another Jesus whom we have not preached, or if you receive a different spirit which you have not received, or a different gospel which you have not accepted—you may well put up with it!" (2 Cor. 11:4). Paul wants to convince the Corinthians to abandon a view of the ministry that is shaped by a godless society's standards and values. As he explains this intent to them, "We do not commend ourselves again to you, but give you opportunity to boast on our behalf, that you may have an answer *for those who boast in appearance and not in heart*" (5:12). He calls into question the accepted notions of outward appearance and he promotes an understanding of true wisdom and power.

Paul's dedication to a cruciform model of ministry is indisputable, yet it seems that few pastors would be inclined to emulate it—and probably few churches would want a pastor who did. It remains an uncomfortable model. In a previous chapter, we mentioned how the influence of worldly culture can affect the way in which church leaders and their gifts are evaluated. For example, the nature of authority today is typically linked to projecting personal strength and charisma. Consequently, pastors might strive to downplay or conceal their weaknesses because they struggle to see how God can employ their shortcomings to accomplish His divine purpose. Indeed, pastors can at times be paralyzed by notions of their inadequacy and might use a "lack of giftedness" as an excuse not to engage fully in the various works of ministry that God sets before them. Yet God can use people of all skill levels in caring for His church, provided that they cultivate a dependence on His Spirit and grace.

While Paul shows how Christ's power can reside in an outwardly weak ministry, there is also an implied warning about the spiritual danger of self-reliance. When a pastor has undeniable gifts in preaching or counseling or leadership, and he does a few significant things to build up the church, he may begin to think that congregational life depends largely on his important contributions. For a pastor, the temptation of arrogance is ever prowling. But the cruciform model of ministry means that he must remain content with the role of a servant, not absorbing worldly standards of successful leadership or seeking prestige and personal affirmation. Rather, grateful service of Christ and His gospel must be expressed by a pastor's wholehearted and selfless service for his congregation. This is a truth that becomes abundantly clear in Paul's extensive recounting of his sufferings in ministry.

Paul's Sufferings in Ministry

I do not know if pastors complain more than anyone else, but from personal experience I'll admit that a pastor is tempted to grumble. A pastor may be inclined to complain to his colleagues, friends, and family about the long hours spent preparing edifying sermons every week, about the loneliness of leadership, or about cranky church members who need to be handled with care. In the first place, a pastor should remember that a complaining spirit is not pleasing to God (Phil. 2:14). What is more, a pastor ought to remember the ultimate purpose of any ministerial struggles: they are for Jesus's sake and for the comfort and salvation of His people.

This truth resounds in 2 Corinthians. While his opponents loved to highlight their notable outward qualities, Paul is keen to speak of personal weaknesses and sufferings. He considered hardships not only to be a fundamental part of life in Christ (see, e.g., Rom. 8:17), but as inevitable in ministry (cf. 2 Cor. 4:8–10). Adversities will be basic to the work of a pastor; as Paul outlines the nature of ministry in 2 Corinthians 6:4–5, "In all things we commend ourselves as ministers of God: in much patience, in tribulations, in needs, in distresses, in stripes, in imprisonments, in tumults, in labors, in sleeplessness, in fastings."

The importance of this theme is clear already from the letter's first chapter, where Paul writes, "For we do not want you to be ignorant, brethren, of our trouble which came to us in Asia: that we were burdened beyond measure, above strength, so that we despaired even of life" (1:8). Paul has recently endured a serious peril that he relates directly to the spiritual welfare of the Corinthians: "Now if we are afflicted, *it is for your consolation and salvation*" (v. 6). Here again is Paul's conviction that God can use his suffering for the benefit of the Corinthians. Paul had suffered, and God the Father had comforted Paul in his affliction, a divine comfort that was now being shared with the Corinthians. He would always be willing to suffer while ministering to his churches because he was confident that it would be for their progress (cf. 1 Cor. 4:10–13).

In this spirit Paul boasts about the experiences of his ministry throughout 2 Corinthians, and especially in chapters 10–13. Because the notion of boasting can easily be misunderstood as self-aggrandizing conceit, Paul's words should be seen against the backdrop of his opponents' claims. As noted in a previous chapter, they portrayed themselves as superior to the apostle in speech, spiritual experiences, and devotion to the Corinthians. Paul refuses to compare himself to them (10:12–13), and even says he is a fool when he does boast (12:11). And far from priding himself in the impressive aspects of his ministry—of which there were surely many!—he exults in those things that show him to be a weak servant of the powerful Christ. His words in 2 Corinthians 11:30 are thematic for the entire letter: "If I must boast, I will boast in the things which concern my infirmity."

And so Paul recounts his sufferings with lists of past and present afflictions. For instance, referring again to his rivals, he asks: "Are they ministers of Christ?—I speak as a fool—I am more: in labors more abundant, in stripes above measure, in prisons more frequently, in deaths often" (11:23). Scholars have pointed out that in Greco-Roman rhetoric, such "catalogs of tribulation" were not uncommon. Writers would detail the misfortunes suffered by political leaders or philosophers in order to demonstrate the integrity of their character, for it was held that hardships revealed the authenticity of one's virtue. Paul seems to adopt this practice in describing his many travails in 2 Corinthians 11: "In journeys often, in perils of waters, in perils of robbers, in perils of my own countrymen, in perils of the Gentiles, in perils in the city, in perils in the wilderness, in perils in the sea, in perils among false brethren" (v. 26). This was the hazardous life to which Christ had called him as a minister of His gospel.

He further recounts his difficulties: "From the Jews five times I received forty stripes minus one" (v. 24). According to Acts, the Jews also stoned him, while at other times he was beaten, whether by mobs or by Roman soldiers. What is more, "three times I was shipwrecked" (v. 25), says Paul, because he was frequently traveling throughout the Mediterranean region to build up the churches. After one of these shipwrecks, he says that for "a night and a day I have been in the deep" (v. 25), probably clinging to a piece of wreckage in the open water and desperately hoping for rescue. Just one month of this kind of suffering would probably make a pastor think seriously about a career change, but Paul endured it, year after year.

Paul expects that some people will accuse him of exaggerating, so he vows, "The God and Father of our Lord Jesus Christ, who is blessed forever, knows that I am not lying" (v. 31). Some of these tribulations were known only to a few, or only to Paul, but even when he suffered alone and in silence, God saw every moment. Even so, this is not about how Paul was so resilient, that he was able to "take a licking and keep on ticking." Instead, it revealed his weakness. Because if you are often in prison, or in bed recovering from the latest beating, you are not going to feel like an effective pastor. If you are always exhausted, hungry, and anxious, you are not going to expect much from your preaching. If you are always in peril, you likely will not be very self-assured. But Paul says that in spite of all this torment and adversity, God is using him for great things. As he writes about his ministry in 2 Corinthians 4:7, "We have this treasure in earthen vessels, that the excellence of the power may be of God and not of us." The high privilege of new covenant ministry had been bestowed on Paul, yet he sees himself as an "earthen vessel," like the easily breakable and soon-discarded jars that were used for common household purposes. The weak and suffering apostle was a worthless container in himself, but this caused the value of "his" treasure to appear more distinctly.

Considering the vast catalog of his tribulation, he wanted the Corinthians to say, "How could Paul ever accomplish what he did? He was so fragile and almost constantly distressed, yet he kept going." And then the attention simply could not fall on him, but on the excellence of the Lord: on His grace, His strength, and His faithfulness. Ministry was never dependent on Paul and his abilities, for he could do nothing apart from Christ (cf. John 15:5). Instead, when Paul was at his weakest, the Lord's strength was most evident. This still ought to be the weak pastor's boast, that he daily depends on Christ and humbly points others to Him.

Paul's Thorn

In chapter 12, Paul's boasting shifts from his trials and weaknesses to visions and revelations. No doubt the first and most important revelation was on the road to Damascus when the risen Jesus confronted him and changed his life's entire course (Acts 9:1–9; cf. Acts 22:6–11; 26:12–20). Paul had also seen a vision of a man from Macedonia urging him to come and help (16:9–10) and he had received other heavenly messages (18:9). Now he relates how he had also been allowed to have a glimpse into heaven: "I know a man in Christ who fourteen years ago—whether in the body I do not know, or whether out of the body I do not know, God knows—such a one was caught up to the third heaven" (2 Cor. 12:2). Paul relates this experience in the third person and describes it opaquely, reluctant to share things that were too sacred to be divulged. He was immensely privileged to have such an experience, yet he downplays this event to prevent anyone from misunderstanding his intent in mentioning it. Notably, it took place fourteen years ago, and this seems to be the first time Paul shares it with the Corinthians! Rather than trumpet this spectacular experience, he prefers that people evaluate him for his continued and demanding work among the churches.

And so after speaking of his vision, Paul immediately returns to the theme of personal weakness. He speaks about how "a thorn in the flesh was given to me," an affliction that he considers to be "a messenger of Satan" and something he has asked God to remove (vv. 7–8). The nature of Paul's thorn has been the subject of much speculation. It has been suggested that the thorn was a form of spiritual trouble, such as a besetting temptation, or it was the ongoing threat of persecution, or it was some physical or mental ailment. More important than its exact identity is Christ's answer to Paul's request to remove the thorn: "My grace is sufficient for you, for My strength is made perfect in weakness" (v. 9). Christ affirms that He can powerfully use human weakness, leading Paul to this hard-fought conclusion: "Therefore most gladly I will rather boast in my infirmities, that the power of Christ may rest upon me" (v. 9). Again, it is when Paul is weak—persecuted, insulted, humiliated, poor, sick, despised, even unloved by his own converts—that Christ's strength becomes most visible. Because through Christ, the weak Paul is enabled to continue faithfully and joyfully in the work of ministry.

The thorn was thus like every other ministerial hardship in being a reason for Paul to point people toward the glorious Lord and His all-sufficient grace. Paul's many and diverse weaknesses mean that great things should be expected not from lowly human servants but from the Savior! It is out of this conviction that Paul is able to view all his ministerial sufferings in a remarkably positive light: "We are hard-pressed on every side, yet not crushed; we are perplexed, but not in despair; persecuted, but not forsaken; struck down, but not destroyed" (2 Cor. 4:8–9). In trouble he fixes his eyes on the power of Christ and he encourages others to do the same, including those pastors today who are acutely aware of their personal weaknesses and burdened by the labors of daily caring for the church.

The Sufferings of Ministry

Despite Paul's hopefulness throughout 2 Corinthians, this is a truth that few seminaries will ever include in their recruitment drives: ministry will involve suffering! It is painful and uncomfortable, but true: struggling in ministry cannot be avoided. For instance, if you are a pastor, you probably have had the experience of coming home from an elders' meeting or a pastoral visit and knowing that once again you are not going to sleep very well. There is too much on your mind as you think about, agonize over, and pray for the people you are trying to help. The lack of sleep may mean a low-grade headache and bags under your eyes in the morning, but it is actually not a bad thing. Paul says that if someone genuinely cares about others and adopts a cruciform model of ministry, this is to be fully expected.

For as Paul reaches the end of his long list of sufferings, he says: "Besides the other things, what comes upon me daily: my deep concern for all the churches" (11:28). He describes it as a heavy burden on him, something that constantly weighs down his heart. It is understandable why he had a "deep concern for all the churches," for he was a mobile minister, wanting to go wherever the gospel had not been preached. God used him effectively for this work, but it came with the anxiety of leaving behind groups of new believers in many places. These groups were often fairly unorganized, occasionally distressed, and sometimes had just an elementary grasp of the faith—to say nothing of all the tensions and challenges of being a holy people trying to live in the midst of a pagan world. So Paul understandably wrestled with apprehensions and worries about his converts. He gives a glimpse of this struggle in 2 Corinthians 7:5: "We were troubled on every side. Outside were conflicts, *inside were fears*."

Paul cares intensely for the people of Christ, so when they face a challenge, it personally affects him. He describes his "deep concern" in 2 Corinthians 11:29: "Who is weak, and I am not weak?" There were some believers who were feeble in faith, prone to periods of doubting, and unsure of God's will in certain situations. When Paul heard about those believers in the churches who struggled with their faith and service, he worried about them. Though he was absent from them, he longed to give help and guidance.

He continues, "Who is made to stumble, and I do not burn with indignation?" (v. 29). One can imagine Paul receiving reports about serious sin in the congregations—and of this Corinth was a prime example. The people he had once pastored were now stealing money, sneaking back to the prostitutes, and getting drunk. When he heard this, Paul could not shrug indifferently, but he felt it keenly, as if it was his own stumbling. It made him upset, and he wanted to assist them in the battle against sin, to pray with them, and to admonish and encourage them. Daily this was another suffering that afflicted him: "a deep concern for all the churches."

Paul here gives voice to something that many pastors can relate to as they carry out a task that can be all-consuming. For a pastor, close engagement with people can take its toll. It is likely that the board of elders—and perhaps even the pastor's wife—doesn't know just how much a devoted pastor thinks of his congregation, takes on their struggles, and carries them close to his heart. Now, when pastors do this, it is sometimes deemed to be a sign of weakness. An inability to detach oneself from people's struggles and heartaches is considered regrettable, and a pastor might wish to become a little more emotionally detached. It is true that one might avoid this sort of relational pain, but only by surrendering to self-centeredness. The fact is, if a pastor is always focused on himself and his own interests, he probably will not care much for the weak and stumbling people in his congregation. But is Paul's lesson in 2 Corinthians that pastors should avoid a wholehearted investment in other people and strive to be detached and aloof? Absolutely not! If anything, this was the mark of the rival pastors in Corinth, men who were too sophisticated to engage with the struggles of real people. If this kind of weakness set Paul apart from them, then he was glad. As he often insisted, for Christ's sake he would willingly accept suffering in order to help others. So when pastors today echo Paul's anguished words about living with a "deep concern" for the believers, it is an indicator of being engaged in a proper, God-pleasing, and self-sacrificing ministry. It is also entirely consistent with what Paul commands all believers in Romans 12, "Rejoice with those who rejoice, and weep with those who weep" (v. 15).

In Christ's service, a pastor ought to share willingly in the struggles and joys of the people to whom he ministers. Maybe the struggle-sharing happens when a pastor visits a broken family, when he counsels someone with a burden of grief or a load of guilt, or when he gives guidance to a husband and wife who are wrestling with the challenges of marriage. Paul's words warn that it is not easy to get close to people, that it can even be disturbing to hear the heartbreaking stories and see the bitter tears. There is a burden that inevitably gets laid on those who help. Yet it is fitting for pastors to share deeply and personally in the lives of those in his congregation. It might be perceived by some as weakness, but it is a Christlike weakness. And when a pastor is tossing and turning in the early hours of the morning, when he is seeing once again his inability to change someone or his inadequacy to help them, he is hopefully learning to depend ever more on the strong Christ. As 2 Corinthians teaches us, it is through human weakness that God delights to show his power. This is how Paul can say in 2 Corinthians 1:6, "If we are afflicted, it is for your consolation and salvation."

The Dedication of Ministry

From this and previous chapters, it is evident that Paul showed an exemplary sense of devotion in ministering among the Corinthians. Such dedication stands as a humbling yet inspiring example to those in pastoral ministry today. I said that probably every pastor is inclined to complain about aspects of his work. Paul might not have known about long and tedious elders' meetings, but he definitely knew about cantankerous people, and agonizing decisions, and the burden of other people's sins and struggles. So Paul surely understood how any pastor can become half-hearted about certain duties and say, "I'll do it, but only because I have to," or "I'll go, but I won't like it. I don't have a choice, do I?"

Service and self-denial are hard, but a pastor can be willing because he gets to care for those whom Christ bought with His own blood. When a pastor knows the eternal value of a soul, he becomes willing to work hard at protecting and nourishing it. Now, this is not to diminish the real need for pastors to get adequate rest, and to take proper care of their bodies and spirits so that they can continue to serve the Lord with energy and joy. There have been far too many men who have burned out and left the ministry under the strain of constant labor in the church. While they should take time to rest and recharge, pastors should also be prepared to give themselves wholly to the work of caring for Christ's people. And if a pastor feels at times like he is pouring himself out for others, then he should know that he is in good company. This is what Paul did. And more importantly, this is what Jesus did, for His entire life was consecrated to service for the salvation of sinners and the honor of God. Even in the hard and trying times, a pastor can be steadfast because he knows that Christ has given him the great privilege of a meaningful task.

Weak but Strong

Probably every pastor likes to imagine himself being heroic, thinking of himself as extraordinary in service. Paul was unquestionably a remarkable pastor and servant of Christ, as shown by his years of ministry. Comparing himself to his rivals, he speaks about working harder, being in prison more frequently, being flogged more severely, being exposed to death, and struggling with weariness, sleeplessness, hunger, and thirst. But so that no one thinks he is boasting in himself, his catalog of sufferings in 2 Corinthians 11 ends like this: "In Damascus the governor, under Aretas the king, was guarding the city of the Damascenes with a garrison, desiring to arrest me; but I was let down in a basket through a window in the wall, and escaped from his hands" (vv. 32–33). The story is familiar. After coming to the Christian faith, Paul's life was in immediate danger, and the believers in Damascus helped him flee. They put him in a big basket and lowered him out of the city. It is memorable, but it seems curious in the context of 2 Corinthians 11. What is the significance of this? In talking about his suffering, why would he put this last, as the climax of the list? Given the choice, I would take evacuation in a basket over flogging any day!

The apostle wants to demonstrate that he is no hero. In recounting this story, he is probably thinking of a Roman military custom. When the legions would besiege and attack a city, the first soldier up the ladder and over the wall was given great honor, for that was a fine act of bravery! The first one over—if he survived, anyway—might be given a small crown as reward. What about Paul? He was not the first one up, he was the first one out. He did not storm up a ladder in boldness of heart, but he was let down in a basket through a window! To be sure, God delivered him that day. Yet in Paul's eyes, this was an example of personal vulnerability like so many other events of his life. Being dumped out of the city like a common fugitive was not his finest hour, but it didn't matter, for Paul boasts in the things that show his weakness. His rivals might have been outwardly impressive, but Paul would celebrate his fragility. Once more, his personal weakness means that people should expect much from Christ.

As we have said, it is natural to have a Corinthian worldview and to be drawn by charisma and eloquence. We prefer riveting speakers and engaging personalities, while we ourselves will always try to be strong and imagine that we can do great things for God. We want to be the hero—or at the very least, we want to be respectable! But if we are Christ's followers, we first need to be covered in shame. To be sure, a person who admits that he needs rescuing looks like a loser. Yet God says good things come from being humbled. Paul might have been weak, even a basket case, yet God greatly blessed his labors. And knowing the certainty of God's strength, pastors, too, can boast in their weakness. They can admit that they lack the ability to convert people or transform lives or build the church. For when a pastor—and any child of God—is willing to confess his emptiness, he will be more ready to trust in Him.

Recall that this is what Christ said to Paul when he prayed that his thorn be taken away. The thorn no doubt hindered his work, but instead of removing it, Christ said, "My grace is sufficient for you, for My strength is made perfect in weakness!" (12:9). It was all that the Lord needed to say: "Rely on My grace." For that is where the strength resides for every weak pastor. When we stop focusing on what we can accomplish and acknowledge that we cannot do it by ourselves, God begins to show His grace in new and surprising ways. Then a suffering and struggling pastor can say with Paul, "When I am weak, then I am strong" (v. 10).

CHAPTER 8

WORKING WITH A PURPOSE

But we do all things, beloved, for your edification.
—2 CORINTHIANS 12:19

Probably every pastor can at times have a sense of aimlessness in ministry. On dark days, he can wonder: What is it all for? What's the use? There has been so much effort for so few gains. Many months of labor in God's vineyard can seem to produce so little fruit. Pastoral aimlessness can take on a different form, too, where there is a retreat to very modest goals. The pastor is simply focused on getting the various tasks done for another week or surviving another three months until the next vacation. Indeed, the work of ministry can sometimes feel like it is only about the immediate concerns of trying to develop better marriages, teach more discerning entertainment choices, and promote a more diligent study of the Bible. But when you peel back a layer or two, and dig beneath the surface of yet another sermon and one more series of pastoral visits, you will see that there is something greater and more beautiful going on. Pastors are working to make Christ's people ready for His triumphant return! In 2 Corinthians, Paul shows how it is this grand aim and vision that should motivate and shape the pastoral task.

A Purpose-Driven Ministry

Throughout Paul's letter, it is clear that he is moved by a strong sense of purpose. This purpose provides strength to his commitment even when others may have expected him to abandon this difficult congregation to his unscrupulous rivals. Instead, he earnestly desires to continue his work among the Corinthians. Rather than letting their relationship deteriorate further, Paul attempts to reestablish the connection between this congregation and its first pastor. When this relationship is strong and healthy, his goals for the Corinthians will progress toward fulfillment.

In previous chapters we saw how Paul explains to the Corinthians his manner of ministry. If they could correctly understand his work among them, they would gain insight into his pastoral vision and begin to cooperate with his best efforts to care for them, rather than resisting. Among his purposes, he desires that the Corinthians' obedience will be fulfilled (2 Cor. 10:6), that their faith will increase (10:15), that they will hold to the true faith (13:5–6), and that they will be made complete in the day of the Lord (13:9). To these pastoral purposes we now turn, exploring them under three headings: reconciliation to God, spiritual growth, and final perfection.

Purpose 1: Reconciliation to God

Paul came to Corinth with an urgent appeal from God and Christ. While we have already looked at his ministerial identity as an ambassador, his message in this capacity bears further examination. In the midst of his explanation of new covenant ministry (2 Cor. 3–6), the apostle issues this serious call to the Corinthians: "We implore you on Christ's behalf, be reconciled to God" (5:20). Convinced that he represents the heavenly King, Paul relays Christ's words to this congregation. He reminds them of the fundamental reconciliation that God brought about through Christ, how His death on the cross is able to restore sinners to fellowship with their maker. On the one hand, to reject an envoy bringing this message is to reject the one who sent him. Conversely, if the gospel that Paul the ambassador preaches is true, then the Corinthians ought to receive him gladly, for such a reception would be to their everlasting spiritual benefit.

Shortly after 2 Corinthians 5:20, Paul issues an appeal on a similar theme: "We then, as workers together with Him also plead with you not to receive the grace of God in vain" (6:1). Though he hopes for their full reconciliation to God, he acknowledges the possibility that some Corinthians will hear his message "in vain." His exhortation is even more urgent because of the congregation's willingness to listen to "a different gospel" from the rival leaders (11:4). Paul desires that Corinth will be a church that is completely transformed by the message of the cross. Yet his appeal in 2 Corinthians 6:1 suggests that the community is still far removed from the goal he is envisioning. And so, even as Paul defends his ministry, he entreats them, "Examine yourselves as to whether you are in the faith. Test yourselves" (13:5). He urges the Corinthians to consider whether they are maintaining the purity and sincerity of faith in Christ, especially while being under the influence of his misleading opponents.

Reconciliation with God is one of Paul's foundational aims for the Corinthians—perhaps even his primary aim. As a pastor, his essential purpose is to link repentant sinners with God's love in Jesus Christ. In fact, Paul judges that he will have failed the test as a servant of Christ if they do not remain in the faith that he preached (cf. 13:6). The apostle's supreme goal for the church is that the restored bond between God and sinners becomes evident in a persevering faith and active obedience: "For the love of Christ compels us, because we judge thus: that if One died for all, then all died; and He died for all, that those who live should live no longer for themselves, but for Him who died for them and rose again" (5:14–15). Paul wants all the Corinthians to come to know—or rather, become reacquainted with—the Christ whom he had first preached among them.

This pastoral purpose remains primary for those who bring Christ's message. Preaching and teaching the true gospel while urging sinners to be reconciled with God gives a pastor's work an eternally meaningful aim. The task of a pastor is not to occupy himself with sanctified social work, inconsequential conversations, or lighthearted messaging. His work is something that God Himself is eternally interested in, for God desires all those who bear His image to be reconciled to Himself. If a pastor grasps that the triune God desires restored fellowship with sinners, he will be urgent and serious in pointing people to Christ, whether in his pastoral conversations, weekly catechism classes, Sunday sermons, or through any other means.

As we will see below, such pastoral urgency arises out of the awareness of Christ's second coming. One day Jesus will come back to this world with glory and power in order to judge the living and the dead. And all people will be judged by their response to Christ. What did we do with the gospel we heard? How did we respond to the preaching of the Word? Pastors and congregations alike must never overlook or downplay this core message: God has graciously granted the forgiveness of sins and everlasting life to all who accept by true faith the one sacrifice of Christ. This message is where everything else in the pastoral task begins, for saving faith will only be initiated and invigorated with a Christ-centered word (cf. Rom. 10:17). This is why Paul insists so strongly: "I determined not to know anything among you except Jesus Christ and Him crucified" (1 Cor. 2:2). And this is why pastors must continue to have a single-minded focus on preaching and teaching the true gospel of Christ: for the salvation of sinners and the glory of God's name.

Purpose 2: Spiritual Growth

Paul has vigorously defended his ministry among the Corinthians, even suggesting that his past behavior has been exemplary. Nevertheless, he maintains that his purpose is not to exalt himself, but to build up the believers in their faith. He reaffirms this core intention toward the letter's conclusion: "Again, do you think that we excuse ourselves to you? We speak before God in Christ. But we do all things, beloved, *for your edification*," or literally, he says, "for building you up" (2 Cor. 12:19). Using the same key word in 13:10, he speaks of how the Lord has given him authority "for edification" (cf. 10:8). Paul knows that the spiritual growth of the church is a wholly divine and supernatural work. Even so, as "workers together with [God]" (6:1), he sees that he and other true pastors are tasked with building up the believers in their faith and obedience.

The language of building in 2 Corinthians is reminiscent of what Paul wrote in his first letter. There he spoke of his involvement in the community's construction: "According to the grace of God which was given to me, as a wise master builder I have laid the foundation, and another builds on it" (1 Cor. 3:10). In the following verses he develops this building image, and emphasizes how anyone involved in spiritual construction is directly accountable to God: "For no other foundation can anyone lay than that which is laid, which is Jesus Christ. Now if anyone builds on this foundation with gold, silver, precious stones, wood, hay, straw, each one's work will become clear; for the Day will declare it, because it will be revealed by fire; and the fire will test each one's work, of what sort it is. If anyone's work which he has built on it endures, he will receive a reward" (vv. 11–14).

In the Greco-Roman world, the "master builder" (v. 10) was an architect of high position. He accepted responsibility for the building's overall design, its site preparation, its workforce, and its actual construction from beginning to completion. For a master builder, laying the foundation was always a vital step in the erection of a building. Therefore, it was necessary that he adhere to the plan from the start or he would be exposed as incompetent. In the same spirit, Paul affirms that working with God's blueprint for his ministry—not a human and socially informed standard—is essential. He will lay the right foundation, which is Jesus Christ, and any further church-building will need to be carefully tested according to Christ's Word. And as a master builder of the church, Paul has a clear conception of his project. He seeks not only the spiritual edification of individual Christians, but the upbuilding of the entire congregation. If by God's grace such a project can be accomplished in Corinth, then one of Paul's chief purposes will be met. But in order to do so, certain areas of spiritual growth will need attention.

While Paul professes his deep love for the Corinthians, even to the point of being willing to suffer and die for their benefit

(2 Cor. 7:3), he does not ignore their shortcomings and imperfections. One of his key aims is to change the Corinthians' system of values. We have previously seen how the congregation was badly influenced by the cultural assumptions of that time. We have also explored how Paul counteracts this by framing his ministry on a cruciform model, asserting that he will perform self-sacrificial service for the good of the church. As a pastor, he relies on Christ's power and example and he rejects any dependence on personal strength or ability. It is these same principles that he wants the Corinthians to apply to themselves so that they are transformed into the likeness of Christ "from glory to glory" (3:18). Conformity to Christ will be expressed through such things as their excellence in giving to support the needy (8:1–12), their continued growth in faith (10:15), and their full obedience to God (10:6).

Growth in giving. Paul persists in his pastoral efforts so that the congregation can "abound in everything" (8:7). Developing their gifts would be not only for the Corinthians' benefit, it would also enable them to bless other churches. For instance, Paul desires that the congregation will generously contribute to the support of the famine-stricken Judean churches: "But as you abound in everything—in faith, in speech, in knowledge, in all diligence, and in your love for us—see that you abound in this grace also" (v. 7). Renewing their generous giving to the collection would be a solid proof that God's transforming grace was active among them.

Growth in faith. Besides seeing them demonstrate generosity toward other Christians, Paul has another objective in working for the Corinthians' spiritual growth. Because of its unique location on the Mediterranean, Corinth was an ideal place from which the gospel could be spread to other areas of the Roman Empire. This was Paul's wish, expressed in 2 Corinthians 10:15–16: "Having hope, that as your faith is increased, we shall be greatly enlarged by you in our sphere, to preach the gospel in the regions beyond you." When he is sure that the congregation's faith is well-grounded, he longs for an opportunity to carry his missionary work from Corinth into new areas. He speaks of this expansion of God's grace in 4:15, "For all things are for your sakes, that grace, *having spread through the many,* may cause thanksgiving to abound to the glory of God." Through the Corinthians' testimony and example, he hopes that more people will become acquainted with God's grace in Christ. Such an expansion of his ministry will only be possible, however, if the congregation remains faithful to God and renews the connection to its Christ-preaching pastor.

Growth in obedience. The increasing transformation of the Corinthians into Christ's image would also be evident in their complete obedience to God (10:6). Paul wants his congregation to become more like Jesus in holiness, love, knowledge, and humble service. Such growth was to be motivated by grateful reverence for God's grace in Christ; as Paul exhorts, "Having these promises, beloved, let us cleanse ourselves from all filthiness of the flesh and spirit, *perfecting holiness in the fear of God*" (7:1). He is hopeful that the Corinthians will be moved to a purer commitment to Christ by hearing and being reminded of His precious promises of salvation.

For pastors today, it ought to remain an essential goal that they would see in their congregation an enhanced conformity to Christ. Any pastor will recognize in his church that many things could be better, and so many areas of its spiritual life need to be built up. For example, is there complacency and worldliness? Is there a lack of neighbor love? Or has the precious truth of baptism or substitutionary atonement been forgotten? Has corporate worship become an empty tradition, or personal prayer a meaningless ritual? There is no doubt that a pastor will see many matters to which he must give attention in his work. And so he should.

But by God's grace, a pastor will also see that his congregation is one of the triune God's marvelous building projects. God is taking sinful people with many flaws and He is restoring them through the Spirit of Christ. God is busy turning sinners into saints and resurrecting a people who once were dead. Pastors are often privileged to see good things happening in the church, whether among the children or the older folks, or anyone in between. There is enthusiasm, devotion, an active communion of saints, generosity, and faithfulness. When pastors see this evidence of transformation, they are reminded that the church is right in the middle of its sanctification. God is not yet done, for He wants His people stronger still: stronger in their knowledge of Scripture, bolder in their witness to the world, brighter in holiness, and firmer in communion. The transformation "from glory to glory" will always be gradual, but it should always be pressing forward.

Anyone in the building industry knows that a construction project can take a long time, for there are almost always unforeseen snags and delays that postpone the completion date. This is also true for the church. Being built up as a congregation takes time because pastors and churches alike are hindered by their sinfulness, hampered by a lack of unity, and impeded by ignorance or immaturity. There may be a delay in growth because of the church leadership's foolish mistakes, or because of the world's hostility, or because of the devil's effective temptations. This is one of the reasons that Christ graciously gives us pastors. When a church is fatigued and frustrated with a lack of progress, a faithful pastor will encourage and exhort with God's Word. No matter how long construction takes, he will aim to keep himself and everyone else based firmly on the only foundation, which is Jesus Christ.

Every congregation is a work in progress that one day will be finished to perfection. The church is like the shell of a building that you see downtown, covered in scaffolding. Looking at the ungainly pile of girders and concrete blocks and the sign out front that boasts the anticipated completion date, you wonder if it will ever get done. Yet two years later you walk past, and there is a sparkling glass building eighty stories tall, fully completed and occupied! When we think about the church "under construction," what is its anticipated completion date? The day of Christ's return! So pastors know that they and their congregations have a definite day for completion and that, until then, spiritual growth and development need to continue.

Already now Christ is working, and He has promised to bring the church to its goal.

Purpose 3: Final Perfection

Paul wrote 2 Corinthians with the immediate aim of restoring the relationship between the congregation and himself, but his ultimate purpose lay far beyond the present time. He wanted to bring the believers to final perfection at Christ's return. Already in 1 Corinthians Paul voiced this pastoral aim, declaring that Jesus "will also confirm you to the end, that you may be blameless in the day of our Lord Jesus Christ" (1:8). His eschatological vision is likewise apparent in 2 Corinthians 1:13–14, where he asserts, "Now I trust you will understand…that we are your boast as you also are ours, *in the day of the Lord Jesus.*" He speaks of the coming day of scrutiny when all people will be tested for their faithfulness to Christ and His Word. Despite all the troubles that have afflicted their relationship, Paul is yet confident that the veracity of their faith will be proven on that day when he will boast in them, even as they boast in their devoted pastor.

For this great purpose Paul continues to work among the Corinthians. It is also his prayer for them: "And this also we pray, that you may be made complete" (13:9). As noted earlier, Paul frequently prays to God for his congregations with specific requests. For the Philippians he prays for an increase in love and discernment (Phil. 1:9). For the Ephesians he prays for growth in knowledge (Eph. 1:17–18). And for the Corinthians he prays for *completion.* The Greek word for "completion" can be translated as "to put in a fit state," "to restore," or even "to perfect." Paul longs for them to reach a real maturity of faith so that they can be fully ready for Christ's second coming. Similarly, he writes in 2 Corinthians 11:2, "For I am jealous for you with godly jealousy. For I have betrothed you to one husband, *that I may present you as a chaste virgin to Christ.*" In an earlier chapter we saw this as an example of Paul's parental pastoring. With all the affection of a father who is fiercely protective of the integrity of his daughter, Paul wants to see the church of Corinth eternally united to Christ in the most intimate of bonds. It is this goal of the final union with Christ that makes Paul's present work truly meaningful.

Final perfection was not his pastoral purpose for the Corinthians alone. For instance, he writes to the Philippians that he was "confident of this very thing, that He who has begun a good work in you will complete it *until the day of Jesus Christ*" (Phil. 1:6). Likewise, to the Colossians he speaks of carrying out his ministry of warning and teaching so "that we may present every man perfect in Christ Jesus" (Col. 1:28). For Paul, this is what makes all his ministerial sufferings endurable and even worthwhile: the reality of a beautiful eternity beyond the present circumstances. Indeed, his current hardships are insignificant when compared to the coming glory. Few observers would have thought that Paul possessed a glorious ministry, yet he considers the spectacular future for him and the church to be certain: "For our light affliction, which is but for a moment, is working for us a far more exceeding and eternal weight of glory" (2 Cor. 4:17). This hope gave him a sure confidence, one that was based on the intrinsic splendor of Christ's gospel and kingdom. The glory for which Paul was working was not an impossibly distant destination but was actually getting closer each day (cf. 1 Cor. 10:11; 2 Cor. 6:2). Such an awareness shapes Paul's view of his ministerial hardships, for instead of avoiding them, he embraces suffering as necessary for the unfolding of God's plan in the last days.

The deep affection that Paul has for the Corinthians also causes him to yearn for their final salvation. Indeed, the relationship that he has with the Corinthians in the present is one that he hopes will continue into a blessed eternity. In chapter 4 Paul writes about "knowing that He who raised up the Lord Jesus will also raise us up with Jesus, *and will present us with you*" (2 Cor. 4:14). He looks forward to seeing the resurrected Corinthians in the presence of God and Christ, when Paul's relationship with this church will no longer suffer any of the effects of brokenness, and when they all will enjoy an unspeakable bliss. This is comparable to the hope that Paul cherishes in his other letters, the longing to see "his" believers on the day of Christ. As he affirms to the Thessalonian church, "For what is our hope, or joy, or crown of rejoicing? Is it not even you in the presence of our Lord Jesus Christ at His coming? For you are our glory and joy" (1 Thess. 2:19–20). As pastor and congregation, their eternal destinies are closely intertwined.

Paul's ultimate goal for the Corinthians can continue to give pastors today not only a certain sense of hope but also a firm purpose. In the first place, ministers of the gospel can cherish the hope that while churches are always works in progress on this side of eternity, one day they will be completed. As the handiwork of the triune God Himself, the church is a project that will definitely be finished to perfection. Despite the pervasive effects of sin, God's saving purpose in Christ is unshakably firm. Pastors may hold on to the hope that Christ is busy perfecting His people, that He is preparing believers for their arrival at a place that does not know sin and brokenness. It will be a place of perfect fellowship between God and His people, and a place of perfect unity among all believers.

In the second place, pastors can imitate Paul's purpose in preparing believers for the return of Christ. This expectation gave an urgency to his work in the congregation of Corinth as he pastored and preached to them. Christians still await the final judgment—indeed, it is closer now than in the time of Paul—with the consequence that pastoral ministry must continue to look steadily toward the day of Christ. There should remain in preaching, teaching, and counseling an element of eschatological urgency as pastors call their congregations to be reconciled to God through Christ. It is good for a pastor to periodically ask himself, Am I preaching every Sunday with the right note of urgency? By my teaching and my visiting, am I getting people ready to meet their maker, ready to appear before the Savior and Judge?

This eternal vision means that pastors should not look for instant results or expect perfect conclusions here below. Life can be terribly messy and broken, and it is not all going to get cleaned up and straightened out before Christ returns. Not that pastors should abandon all notions of spiritual progress or growth, but they should remember God's long horizon. More than anything, a pastor wants his congregation to share by faith in Christ's gracious gift of life everlasting. It can take a long time to get there, and it can require an immense amount of trying work, but God's promised reward in Christ is sure: "For all the promises of God in Him are Yes, and in Him Amen, to the glory of God through us" (2 Cor. 1:20). Through Christ, pastors can always work with a sure sense of hope and a firm purpose.

Parting Words

After all the abuse that he had endured from the Corinthians, and in view of all the spiritual flaws they demonstrated, one might expect Paul to slip in some parting criticism with the last words of his letter. But instead, Paul affirms the strength of the congregation. "For we are glad when we are weak and you are strong" (13:9). This is a surprising way to describe these divided, disloyal, and decadent believers: "you are strong." Yet by now we understand that Paul has a different way of looking at things. If he calls the Corinthians "strong," he is not thinking of anything that could be attributed to their hard work or noble character. How could they ever be strong but in the Lord?

Precisely what was true for Paul was true for these Corinthians. Outwardly, they were weak and afflicted by many failings—they would never get a prize for being upstanding Christians. Paul says that he was still afraid he would find in Corinth "contentions, jealousies, outbursts of wrath, selfish ambitions, backbitings, whisperings, conceits, tumults" (12:20). This was the reality of their sinful condition, as it is the reality of any church in any place. Yet Paul says that he is grateful for their progress and strength, because despite all their imperfections and sins, this congregation remains the bride of Christ. Even these troubled and troubling Corinthians were God's people, holy and dearly loved. In Christ, the weak are strong.

In carrying out his work as a pastor, Paul has the awareness that he himself is but one more child of God on the long and difficult road to eternity. Paul's words throughout this letter suggest his confidence in personally having attained maturity in Christ. Yet Paul understands that all believers, whether an apostle-pastor or congregational member, are still traveling the path to glory. In these closing words he reminds them of his weakness: "We are glad *when we are weak*" (13:9). His own fragile and broken life bears ample witness to the fact that he is still on a journey toward perfection in the presence of Christ. Earlier Paul assured the congregation of his own life's goal and purpose: "Therefore we make it our aim, whether present or absent, to be well pleasing to Him. For we must all appear before the judgment seat of Christ, that each one may receive the things done in the body, according to what he has done, whether good or bad" (5:9–10). With this eternal aim, the weak pastor will continue his humble work of ministry for Christ's sake.

TRAVELING FROM THE FIRST CENTURY TO TODAY

Not that we are sufficient of ourselves to think of anything as
being from ourselves, but our sufficiency is from God, who also
made us sufficient as ministers of the new covenant, not of the
letter but of the Spirit; for the letter kills, but the Spirit gives life.
—2 CORINTHIANS 3:5–6

Where are they now? Whatever happened to so-and-so? These are questions people like to ask about the pop singers and film stars of bygone decades. Now that we have arrived at the end of our exploration of Paul's relationship with the congregation at Corinth, our thoughts return to the Corinth of the first century. After the writing and reading of 2 Corinthians, what happened to this church that had for so long been the object of Paul's loving pastoral care? How was Paul's pleading, affectionate, and sometimes pointed and ironic letter received?

This is certainly the question that is suggested by the end of his letter. It is clear from his own words that Paul's pastoral work among the Corinthians remained unfinished. Nevertheless, other passages in the New Testament suggest that there were some positive results that arose directly out of Paul's pastoral strategy in the writing of 2 Corinthians. When he wrote his letter to the Romans, he could affirm that his work in the eastern Mediterranean—including the city of Corinth—was completed, and so he could move on to ministry in new areas, such as Spain (Rom. 15:23–24). In the same letter, he expressed gratitude that the region of Achaia was joining with Macedonia in contributing to the collection for the Jerusalem church (v. 26), the ministry of mercy that Paul had worked hard to encourage among the Corinthians. These positive fruits suggest that there had not been a lasting rupture between the Corinthians and the apostle, but that they had responded positively to his words of admonition and exhortation. We also see that some of Paul's Corinthian friends remained faithful to the apostle. For instance, Paul spent three winter months in Corinth in AD 56–57 as the guest of Gaius at a time when he was writing the letter to the Romans (Rom. 16:23; cf. 1 Cor. 1:14). For all the trouble that he had experienced there, Corinth was still a welcoming place for him. Admittedly, this is meager evidence. But Paul seems to have met a few of his specific goals in connection with the Corinthians. His careful teaching and affectionate pleading had produced some fruit in the church at Corinth.

But what about Corinth's history beyond the horizon of the New Testament? From the history of the early church we learn that after some years the internal struggles in the Corinthian congregation continued. The success that Paul achieved with this letter seems to have been short-lived. Notably, there is a rebuking letter that the church father Clement wrote to believers in Corinth in the late first century AD. Clement was bishop of the church in Rome, which apparently took on the subsequent supervision of the churches in Paul's mission fields. The tone and content of the letter of 1 Clement to the Corinthians suggest that the congregation was again divided and was seemingly in a revolt against its spiritual leaders. For this reason, Clement has to reprimand the Corinthians. It is striking that he even reminds them to read again what the apostle Paul had written in one of his letters to them. These are Clement's reproving words to the volatile congregation:

> Take up the epistle of the blessed Apostle Paul. What did he write to you at the time when the Gospel first began to be preached? Truly, under the inspiration of the Spirit, he wrote to you concerning himself, and Cephas, and Apollos, because

even then parties had been formed among you.... But now reflect who those are that have perverted you, and lessened the renown of your far-famed brotherly love. It is disgraceful...and unworthy of your Christian profession, that such a thing should be heard of as that the most stedfast and ancient Church of the Corinthians should, on account of one or two persons, engage in sedition against its presbyters. (1 Clement 47, in *Ante-Nicene Fathers*, vol. 1)

It is not clear how this admonition was received. After the time of Clement, the congregation at Corinth passes out of the view of the historical record. One can only imagine the trials and travails that marked its continued existence in the post-apostolic age, as the Roman Empire began its inexorable decline.

Reality of Ministry

Seeing the unfinished nature of the work in the church of Corinth is a suitable point of departure for a few final reflections. Reading 2 Corinthians should move us to consider carefully how we will work with these same abiding truths as individual believers and as ministers of the gospel.

The history of the Corinthian congregation reveals that even the apostle Paul had to face his limitations as one of the human servants of Christ. What he said when grappling with the nature of his task again comes to mind, "Who is sufficient for these things?" (2 Cor. 2:16). While the apostle did go on to affirm that it is God who gives all the competence for ministry, the first-century Corinthian situation teaches us to expect that Christian ministry in the present time will be fraught with much weakness and hardship.

The high ideals that are held and the noble goals that are set in the seminary years regularly run up against the hard realities of a broken world and a still-sinful church. In view of these disappointments, questions of personal competence and character can become pronounced for a pastor. There are any number of reasons why a pastor might doubt his ability to lead a congregation effectively and purposefully. Honest self-evaluation might suggest that every area of competency in ministry stands to be improved on: preaching, teaching, counseling, and more. And in each of these areas there probably needs to be an improved ability to relate meaningfully to other people, through understanding them better, sympathizing with them more sincerely, and connecting with them on more than a superficial level.

Then when we hear Paul's glorious exposition of true ministry and we see his frank portrayal of the strained relationship with the Corinthians, this can make the personal burden of the ministerial task seem even heavier. For clearly, it is work that can be intensely difficult. It is hard not to be mentally and emotionally drained by the various hardships and stresses of ministry. It is hard to receive personal criticism, whether the criticism is justified or not. In preaching or in counseling, it is hard not to be unduly influenced by what the congregational members want to hear. It is hard not to hold difficult members at a distance instead of engaging with them. It is hard not to be ensnared by the love of money or the love of praise. It is hard not to look at all the work simply as "things to get done," while forgetting the eternal goal toward which everything is moving. It is immensely hard to be like Jesus Christ in suffering willingly and selflessly for others. How difficult it is to come alongside those who are in need of help and to allow God's power to be displayed through the hardships of the pastor's life and ministry!

Hope for Ministry

Yet the same letter that confronts a Christian pastor with his shortcomings and inadequacies also challenges him to be resolute in imitating Pastor Paul, and in imitating him, to imitate Jesus Christ. For the same letter offers a powerful reminder about the great privilege in being an ambassador of the crucified and risen Christ, in preaching Him boldly and bringing His words meaningfully into the lives of His believers. And the same letter provides the rich encouragement that God is greater than any and every human weakness. For Paul's despondent question in 2 Corinthians 2:16—"Who is sufficient for these things?"—finds its beautifully confident answer in the following chapter: "Not that we are sufficient of ourselves to think of anything as being from ourselves, but our sufficiency is from God, who also made us sufficient as ministers of the new covenant" (3:5–6). In desiring sinners to be reconciled to Himself, God commands that the saving message of Christ be preached and taught and applied in the life of His believers. And God is content to use imperfect human servants in order to carry out this eternally meaningful work.

It is a great reassurance to know that the triune God's reconciling purpose will always prevail, and that He will provide His weak servants with everything required to accomplish this task here on earth. To echo again the often-quoted words of Paul, "Therefore I take pleasure in infirmities, in reproaches, in needs, in persecutions, in distresses, for Christ's sake. For when I am weak, then I am strong" (12:10). For meeting all the responsibilities and challenges of pastoral ministry, Christ will supply superabundant strength and abiding joy. At the same time, Christ will give essential guidance and much-needed encouragement—if we are willing to listen to such wise teachers as Pastor Paul.

SELECTED BIBLIOGRAPHY

The literature on both 2 Corinthians and New Testament models of ministry is vast. The following are works that have been especially helpful in shaping my understanding of gospel ministry in 2 Corinthians and that may be useful to readers who wish to pursue further study of these topics.

Barnett, Paul. *The Second Epistle to the Corinthians.* New International Commentary on the New Testament. Grand Rapids: Eerdmans, 1997.

Best, Ernest. *Paul and His Converts.* Edinburgh: T & T Clark, 1988.

Bruce, F. F. *Paul and His Converts.* Downers Grove, Ill.: InterVarsity, 1985.

Carson, Donald A. *The Cross and Christian Ministry: Leadership Lessons from 1 Corinthians.* Grand Rapids: Baker, 1993.

———. *From Triumphalism to Maturity: An Exposition of 2 Corinthians 10–13.* Grand Rapids: Baker, 1984.

Chadwick, W. E. *The Pastoral Teaching of St. Paul.* Edinburgh: T & T Clark, 1907.

Clarke, Andrew D. *Secular and Christian Leadership in Corinth.* Eugene, Ore.: Wipf & Stock, 2006.

———. *Serve the Community of the Church: Christians as Leaders and Ministers.* Grand Rapids: Eerdmans, 2000.

Fee, Gordon D. *The First Epistle to the Corinthians.* New International Commentary on the New Testament. Grand Rapids: Eerdmans, 1987.

Furnish, Victor Paul. "Theology and Ministry in the Pauline Letters." In *A Biblical Basis for Ministry,* edited by Earl E. Shelp and Ronald Sunderland, 101–144. Philadelphia: Westminster, 1981.

Garland, David E. *2 Corinthians.* New American Commentary 29. Nashville, Tenn.: Broadman & Holman, 1999.

———. "Paul's Apostolic Authority: The Power of Christ Sustaining Weakness." *Review and Expositor* 86 (1989): 371–89.

Harris, Murray. *The Second Epistle to the Corinthians.* New International Greek Textual Commentary. Grand Rapids: Eerdmans, 2005.

Kruse, Colin. *New Testament Models for Ministry: Jesus and Paul.* Nashville, Tenn.: Thomas Nelson, 1985.

Martin, R. P. *2 Corinthians.* Word Biblical Commentary 40. Waco, Tex.: Word, 1986.

McKnight, Scot. *Pastor Paul: Nurturing a Culture of Christoformity in the Church.* Grand Rapids: Brazos, 2019.

Murphy-O'Connor, Jerome. *The Theology of the Second Letter to the Corinthians.* Cambridge: Cambridge University Press, 1991.

Myrick, A. "'Father' Imagery in 2 Corinthians 1–9 and Jewish Paternal Tradition." *Tyndale Bulletin* 47 (1996): 163–71.

Peterson, Brian K. *Eloquence and the Proclamation of the Gospel in Corinth.* Society of Biblical Literature Dissertation Series 163. Atlanta: Scholars Press, 1998.

Savage, Timothy B. *Power through Weakness: Paul's Understanding of Christian Ministry in 2 Corinthians.* Society for New Testament Studies Monograph Series 86. Cambridge: Cambridge University Press, 1996.

Thiselton, Anthony C. *The First Epistle to the Corinthians.* International Greek Textual Commentary. Grand Rapids: Eerdmans, 2000.

Thompson, James W. *Pastoral Ministry according to Paul.* Grand Rapids: Baker Academic, 2006.

Ventura, Rob, and Jeremy Walker. *A Portrait of Paul: Identifying a True Minister of Christ.* Grand Rapids: Reformation Heritage Books, 2010.

Witherington, Ben. *Conflict and Community in Corinth: A Socio-Rhetorical Commentary on 1 and 2 Corinthians.* Grand Rapids: Eerdmans, 1995.